MW00666956

FUNK BASS

by JON LIEBMAN

Foreword by JOHN PATITUCCI

ISBN 0-7935-1620-X

Hal Leonard Publishing Corporation
7777 West Bluemound Road P.O. Box 13819 Milwaukee, WI 53213

TABLE OF CONTENTS

NOTATION LEGEND

T-Slap the string with your thumb

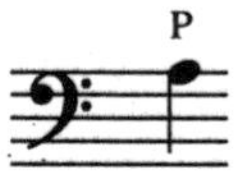

P-Pop the string with your index finger

H-Hammer-on

PO-Pull-off

Slide into a new note after another note has been articulated

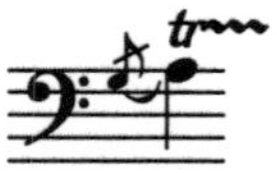
Trill

Shake

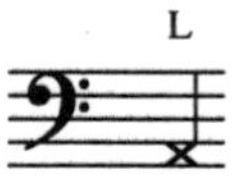

L-Strike the open strings with the fingers of your left hand

Bend the note

FOREWORD

Musicians today have extraordinary demands placed upon them and have been forced into a "sink-or-swim" situation. The fact of the matter is that players are finally realizing that, "If I can't do it, somebody else can — no problem." A sobering thought, to say the least.

Bass players are no exception. A good bass player must be able to read and play in all styles, solo upon request, perform flawlessly in tune, have an impeccable time feel, read minds, be humble, be friendly, smile, thump, walk, strut, swing, shuffle and, for Heaven's sake, relax!

Everyone talks about grooving, i.e., making the music feel good. After all, what good would music be if it didn't groove? Jon couldn't be more right on the money when he says, "groove is everything and everything must groove." Remember: if you're not grooving, you're not playing the bass.

If you have any aspirations of stepping out into the real world, you must know what you're doing, and if you're going to learn to groove on the bass, you might as well learn it right. *Slapping* is still a very popular style of bass playing (as if we didn't already have enough to worry about) and I have never seen a better book from which to learn this style.

Funk Bass is, by no means, just another "licks" book. It explains, in a logical, step-by-step order, what to do and what *not* to do. It is an invaluable resource for learning and understanding what is required and expected from a bass player in today's highly competitive music environment. It also contains excellent information, tips, advice and insight on equipment and practicing, all in a clear, friendly, thorough, yet concise, writing style. Topping it all off is an extensive **Discography** for recommended listening — the longest I've seen in any book of this type. Listening is essential and is at least as important as the exercises you'll practice.

This is the first time I have ever seen so much information compiled into one comprehensive volume. Getting to the point is not always easy to do. Getting the point across is even harder. The point is this: Groove. Plain and simple. Congratulations, Jon. I think you really got the point across beautifully!

I highly recommend Funk Bass to all "slappers" and "wanna-be slappers." It's a "can't-miss!"

God bless you all.

—John Patitucci

John Patitucci is a world-renowned virtuoso of both the electric and acoustic bass. He is also considered one of the pioneers of the electric six-string bass. Mr. Patitucci has been active in the West Coast music scene since 1979, having played with Larry Carlton, Stan Getz, Dave Grusin, Freddie Hubbard, Lee Ritenour, Tom Scott, John Scofield, Wayne Shorter and many others.

John became widely known in 1985 when he became a member of the Chick Corea Elektric and Akoustic Bands, with which he recorded eight albums. He also has recorded three solo albums, entitled ***John Patitucci, On The Corner*** *and* ***Sketchbook****, all on the GRP record label. John remains active in the L.A. studio and club scenes, and is currently developing his career as a solo artist.*

INTRODUCTION

The goal of this book is to introduce the contemporary bassist to the funk style of playing. Many books of this type miss the point of what is required of a bass player. Being able to execute a bunch of fast funk licks may dazzle your friends and relatives, but it won't make your phone ring off the hook from contractors and record producers calling you with work. In the real world, you'll be hired according to how well you understand your role as a bass player and how well you do your job. This book will guide you toward those goals in a logical, step-by-step "real-world" approach.

Chapter 1, **A Word On Practicing**, emphasizes the importance of proper practice habits. It includes discussions on metronomes, drum machines, live drummers, tape recorders, utilizing recordings, attending live concerts and maintaining a music notebook.

Chapter 2 begins illustrating the fundamentals of funk bass playing — how to "slap" and "pop." The emphasis here is on precision and proper execution. The exercises in this chapter are developed into some basic funk patterns in Chapter 3.

Chapter 4 introduces some stylistic elements, such as the "hammer-on," the "pull-off," the slide, the trill, the shake and the bend (no, it's not a dancing lesson!). These are the so-called "tricks of the trade" that will make your playing sound funkier.

The focus in Chapter 5 is on establishing a groove — the most important element of playing the bass. If you're going to get anything at all out of this book, get this: **GROOVE IS EVERYTHING, AND EVERYTHING MUST GROOVE!** I can't over-emphasize the importance of this statement. It holds true for all musicians, but especially for the bass player and the drummer, because they're the ones that really lay down the time and make the music "feel" good.

Once you understand this concept and are comfortable (honestly!) with Chapters 2 through 5 of this book, feel free to have fun with the licks I have included in Chapter 6. They are intended to illustrate different possibilities of the funk style, help you develop your technique and give you ideas for creating your own funk lines. Remember, your job is to groove and support the band. These licks are to be used at your discretion as your taste and musicality dictate. They can work very well as fills within the groove or, of course, for your solos.

It is crucial to be able to play in all keys. Many students of funk bass can really "get down" in one or two keys, but are practically helpless when they have to play for a singer whose song is not in "E" or "A" but in some "weird" key. Because this is so important, I have made sure to include plenty of exercises and licks (and grooves!!!) in all twelve keys. Where other books simply suggest, "try these licks in a few different keys," I felt it was important enough to actually write them out. Of course, you are encouraged to transpose anything in this book into any or all twelve keys. It's good for you! It will help your reading, too.

What's more, the key of "C♯" is not the same as "D♭," nor is "F♯" the same as "G♭," nor "B" the same as "C♭." By the time you get through this book, you'll be able to read and play in any key. Granted, certain keys (like "E" and "A") lend themselves to greater ease and facility on the bass, because of the nature and tuning of the instrument. Also, some keys may be harder to read, but easier to play in, and vice versa. When you come right down to it, there are no such things as "easy" or "hard" keys, only "familiar" keys and "unfamiliar" keys.

The Appendix, **Your Equipment**, provides an overview of the equipment common to funk bass players. It includes information on types of basses, strings, amplifiers, speakers and effects. It is intended to "de-mystify" the myriad of products available to musicians today, and offers insights into how to invest carefully in the proper tools that will best suit *your* needs.

At the end of this book I have included a **Discography**, which is by no means exhaustive, but offers a cross section of some of the greatest funk bassists in music today. It's important that you listen to as much of this music as possible so you understand just exactly what we're trying to do here. If you get a chance to see any of these guys live, don't you dare miss them!

Move slowly and go through this book one step at a time, in order. When you reach the end, you will have learned how to function as a funk bass player and how to lock in with the drummer. You will understand the concept of a proper time feel, and have the ability to create funk bass lines of your own. You will be able to read and play comfortably in all twelve keys. You'll know who to listen to and what to listen for to hear incredible funk bass playing.

In short, you'll have the tools that are required of a great funk bassist. Making grooves "feel" funky comes from lots of listening and practicing. It's no secret that the way to get good at something is to put in the time and effort. It's up to you. You can be the one that producers and contractors like to call. It all comes back to how well you understand your role, how well you do your job and how good of a hustler you are.

Good luck, and remember: GROOVE!!!

J.L.

Chapter 1
A Word On Practicing

"Practice doesn't make perfect. *Perfect* practice makes perfect."
— Vince Lombardi

These words, by the late, internationally renowned coach of the Green Bay Packers, are profoundly true. Whether you're talking about music or football, Mr. Lombardi's philosophy still applies. Even if you spend eight hours a day in the woodshed, you could be wasting your time if you don't have proper practice habits. In this chapter, we'll look at what distinguishes "good" practicing from "bad" practicing, and how to make the most efficient use of the hours you spend honing your funk bass skills.

"Did you say *bad* practicing?" "Does it really exist?"

Absolutely! Do you ever just "wander" around the bass, aimlessly, playing lick after lick? Do you often find yourself charging ahead through bass lines and solos that you already can play inside out? When you practice a part, do you think only of the bass, without considering the interplay between you and the other musicians (the drummer, for one)? Do you practice without a metronome or a drum machine? Or in front of the TV? If you answered yes to any of these questions, you may be found guilty of "bad practicing" and could be subject to eternal banishment from all that's hip, and forced to tap your toes on "one" and "three" for the rest of your life!

When you practice, it's serious business. Create an environment that's conducive to study. Keep distractions out of sight. Find a time when you won't be disturbed. Convince yourself that you're not hungry or thirsty, and get in the proper frame of mind.

My teacher used to have me keep a log of my practice sessions, which was a great help. Get a calendar, in which you'll record nothing but your practice schedules. Every day, take into account how many hours you're going to spend practicing and what you need to work on, then budget your time accordingly. Write down, for example, 30 minutes for scales and arpeggios, 20 minutes for sight-reading, etc. When the time alloted for each segment expires, move on to the next one, checking things off as you go. That way you're constantly chipping away at everything every day, and won't have to worry about three weeks going by without playing any Stu Hamm finger taps, or whatever else may be on your agenda. At the end of the week, take a look at your calendar and see how much practicing you're actually doing, versus how much you *think* you're doing. The results may surprise you.

"Time is of the essence." I don't know who first uttered those words, but they couldn't hold more truth for bassists. When you're practicing by yourself, always use a metronome, or, better yet, a drum machine. Remember: they're your friends! Concentrate not only on playing in time, but with a good time *feel*. A *GREAT* time feel. So what if you know the right changes to 40,000 tunes? Who cares if you can play eighty-bizillion sixteenth notes a minute, or have the "baddest" setup this side of Osaka. ***THE MOST IMPORTANT JOB YOU HAVE AS A BASS PLAYER IS TO GROOVE WITH A GREAT TIME FEEL.*** You may think you're playing in time, but the metronome and drum machine will keep you "honest," so use them.

Another way to work on your time feel is to get together with a good drummer and groove. For hours. Don't just fool around, though. Concentrate on "takin' care o' business." Oh, sure, you can still work on your solo chops, but spend most, if not all, of the time *on* the time. Pick several grooves that you want to work on, and practice them one at a time, over and over, without stopping. Be sure to play in all twelve keys, too. You may want to have your drummer friend program a few grooves into your drum machine, for you to practice with when you're by yourself.

So far, we've got three friends: a metronome, a drum machine and a real live warm body behind the drums. Let's add one more friend to our list: the tape recorder.

Back we go, once again, to the "honesty" category. You think you know what your playing sounds like? Try laying it down on tape and see (hear) if you're right. "Tape recorders don't lie." Recording your playing may reveal many flaws and bad habits of which you may not have been aware. It lets you really zero in on the attack and release of each note, as well as your sustain, intonation, *time feel* and overall sound. A tape recorder can be an invaluable practice tool.

Another great way to practice is to learn bass grooves from records, and then play along with them. Use your tape recorder to compare your line with Marcus Miller's line and see how it measures up. I'm not saying you should try to sound like Marcus, but if you think you're putting all the notes in the right places and it still isn't quite happening, try to pinpoint what it is about your playing that sounds different than the record. Keep in mind though, all the variables involved in creating music, like the player, strings, attack, electronics and effects, plus the fact that Marcus' bass is mixed with all the other sounds on the record. No matter how similar your style is to his, you won't sound like Marcus when you're practicing in your bedroom.

Try to get out to see great players perform as much as possible. In many cases, when you can *see* what they're doing, you'll understand certain bass concepts in a completely different way. If you can go down and talk to them, go ahead. Most people are friendly and they may be able to offer you some insights into bass playing that may encourage you. Live performances are great for incorporating inspiration into your practice sessions.

Finally, keep a music notebook of any new ideas that may hit you. If you hear something while practicing, write it down. Or it might be when you're in the car, or in the shower, or in bed or ... well, you get the idea. This book came about, partially, because I had an idea and didn't want to forget it, so I wrote it down. Then I got another idea. And another. And I wrote those down. After several years of this process, my ideas eventually culminated into this book.

To get the full benefit from keeping a notebook, use it along with your friends, Mr. Drum Machine, Mr. Tape Recorder and your other pals. You may want to write down tempos or other information, too. Your ideas may even turn into tunes that make you rich. So give it a try. You may be surprised at how much creativity you have inside your brain that would have otherwise been lost forever.

Following these guidelines will improve your practicing tremendously. I recommend referring back to this chapter occasionally, when your practice sessions need a little "shot in the arm."

CHAPTER 2
GETTING STARTED

The whole thing is really kind of funny. It all began one day, back in the late sixties, when no drummer could be found for miles around. The bass player had to lay down the time, the groove, the feel and the pocket all by himself, as if he were a bassist and a drummer rolled into one. The "thumb slaps" functioned as the kick drum, and the "finger pops" supplied the backbeat of the snare drum. The rest of the stuff was fills.

The man usually given credit for developing this style of bass playing is Larry Graham, of Sly & The Family Stone and Graham Central Station. Other early innovators include Louis Johnson of The Brothers Johnson, and Bootsy Collins of George Clinton's Parliament Funkadelic.

Throughout the following decade, the idea seemed to catch on like wildfire. The seventies brought us Stanley Clarke, who practically scared everyone to death with his blistering speed (not just with his thumb, but with his fingers, too!). Neil Jason and Will Lee are two other very influential funk players to come out of that period.

The heroes of the eighties were Mark King, Marcus Miller and John Patitucci. Other important players include Victor Bailey, Brian Bromberg, Oscar Cartaya, Nathan East, Jonas Hellborg, Darryl Jones, Tim Landers, John Peña and several others. Who's to say what new names will "pop" up in the nineties? Maybe yours! In the meantime, be sure to use the **Discography** in the back of this book to do some serious listening. It's *SO* important!

Now that you've had a little history lesson, let's begin with the basics (*bassics?*) of funk bass playing, namely, slapping and popping. Since everything else in this book is built upon these techniques, it's crucial that you become proficient and comfortable with them before proceeding any further.

The *Slapping* Technique. "Slapping" simply means hitting the strings with your right thumb. This technique is the foundation of funk bass playing, and must be executed with utmost precision. I find that the most practical spot (and the most comfortable) for the thumb is at the end of the fingerboard at about a forty-five degree angle to the neck of the bass.*

The *Slapping* Technique

Take a look at Exercise 2.1, and try striking the open "E" and the "A" strings with the joint of your right thumb. Start very slowly and deliberately, with your metronome set at quarter note = 60. Concentrate on getting the fullest sound possible, and on striking only one string at a time.

Note: *In order to facilitate more efficient arm movements while slapping the bass, many players wear their basses quite high. If you find you are uncomfortable at first, try shortening your strap a little and see how it feels. It's also important that your bass stay in one position, regardless of whether you're sitting or standing.*

*Many variations exist about where and how to place your thumb. Tony Levin, for example, plays completely differently than, say, Abe Laboriel. Feel free to experiment with the positioning of your thumb. Just make sure the emphasis is on precision of attack and fullness of sound.

Standing Position

Sitting Position

2.1

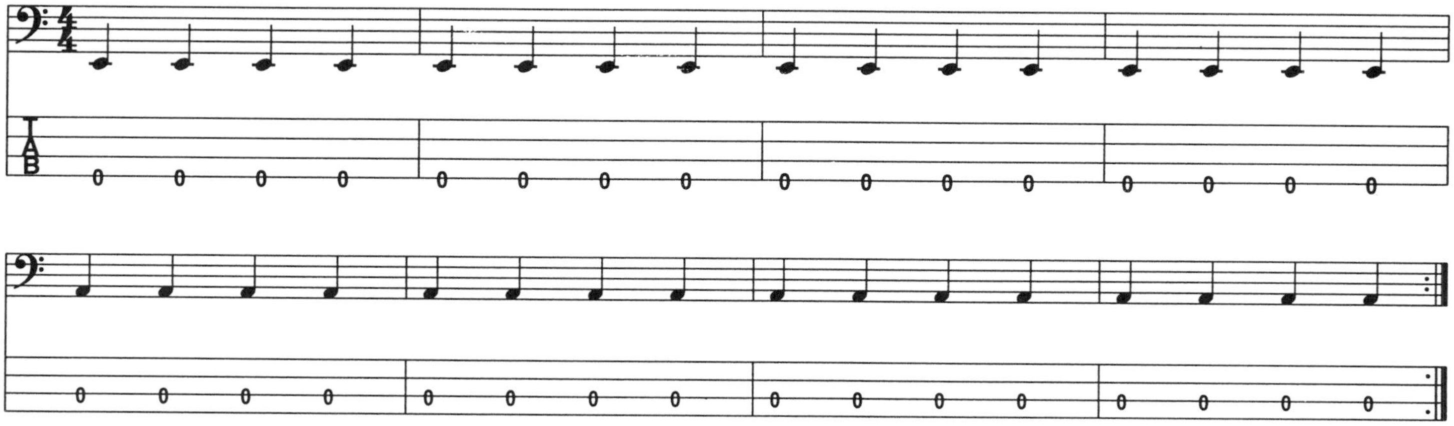

Now let's continue the same exercise, but on the open "D" and "G" strings. Slapping on these two strings is not as common as on the other two strings, but the need does arise occasionally. Besides, we're going to be thorough, alright? In fact, while we're at it, if you've got a five- or six-string bass, practice this exercise on the "B" and "C" strings, as well.

2.2

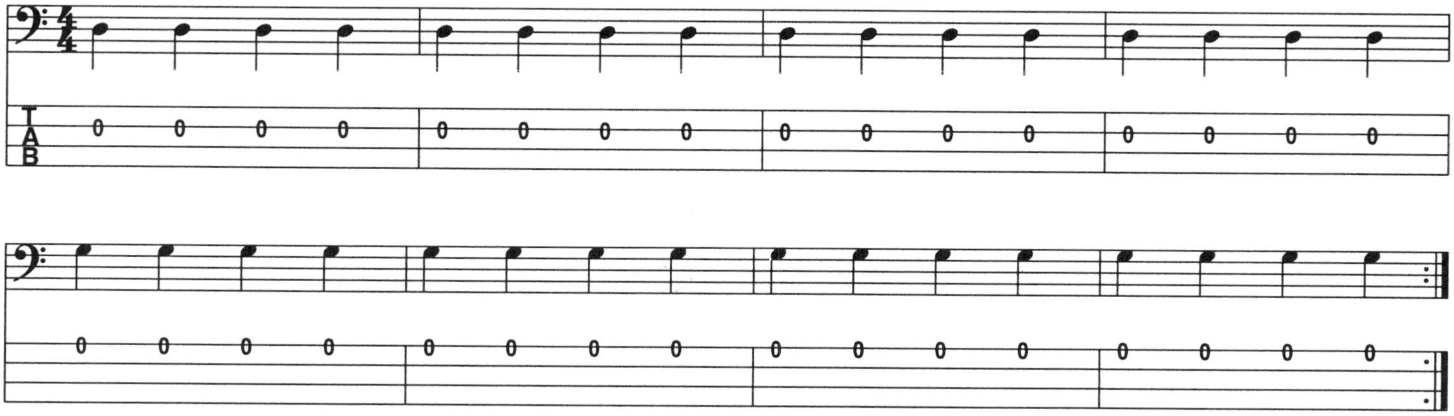

Continue this drill with Exercises 2.3-A through 2.3-F by combining all four strings. Remember: for these exercises, only use open strings. For ALL exercises, use your metronome or drum machine.

2.3 (A)

2.3 (B)

2.3 (C)

2.3 (D)

2.3 (E)

2.3 (F)

Before you go any further, spend some time on Exercises 2.1 through 2.3-F and make sure you're comfortable with them. Try varying the tempos a little and see how it feels (and sounds).

Note: *If you're new to this style of playing, don't try to do too much too soon. Constant pounding on metal round-wound strings can be quite traumatic to your thumb, so make sure you build up your strength and endurance in moderation. If you start to get sore (and most likely you will), take a break and go transcribe a Charlie Parker solo. Before you know it, you'll forget all about your aching thumb!*

Let's add a little rhythm now, as we slowly start getting more musical. Exercises 2.4-A through 2.7-B alternate between the lower three and the upper three open strings. Go through each one and concentrate on playing them all accurately.

The repeat signs don't necessarily mean to play each exercise twice and then move on. As with all studies in this book, if something isn't clear or if you can't play an exercise to your satisfaction, go back and work it through until you're comfortable before going any further.

2.4 (A)

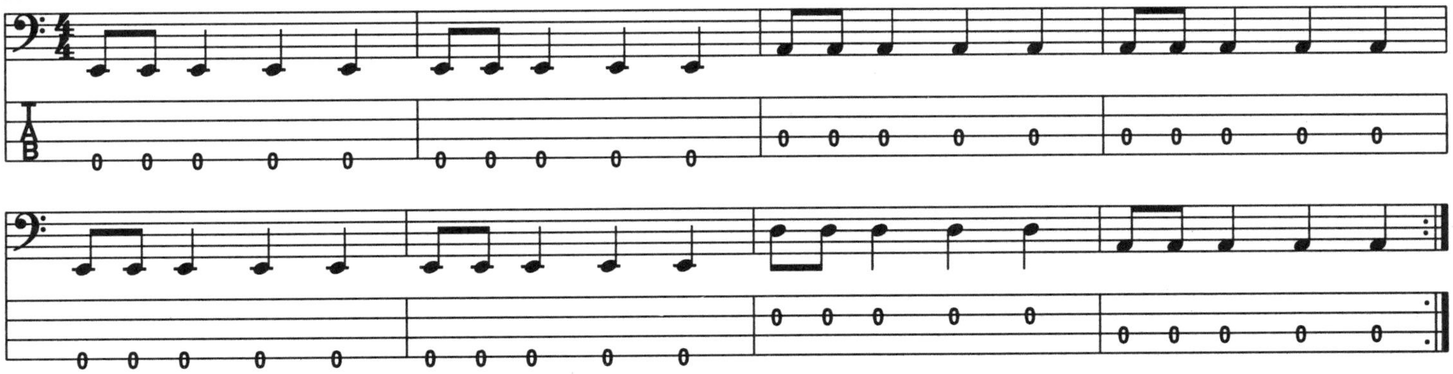

2.4 (B)

Continue this exercise with the following variations in rhythm:

2.5 (A)

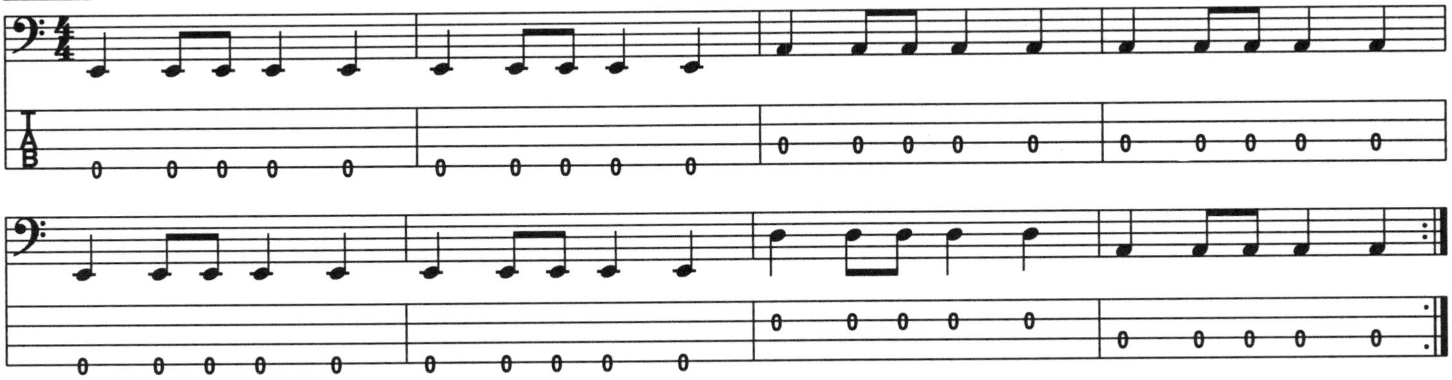

2.5 (B)

2.6 (A)

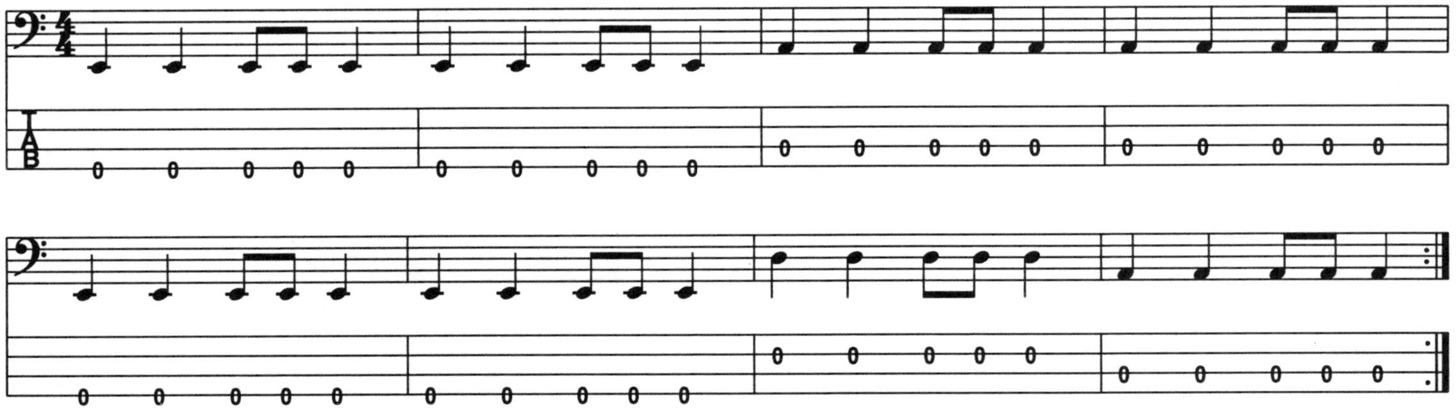

2.6 (B)

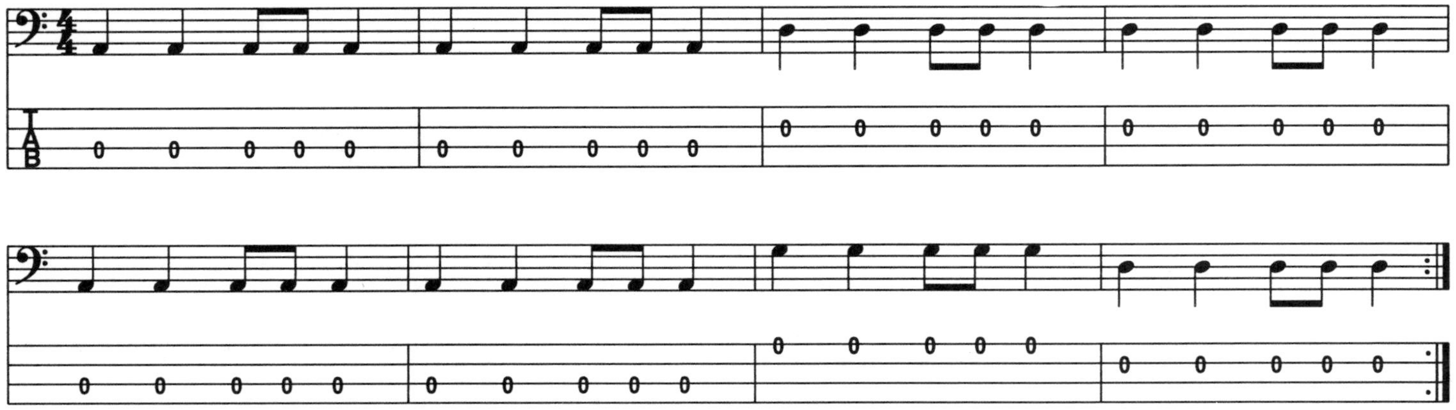

2.7 (A)

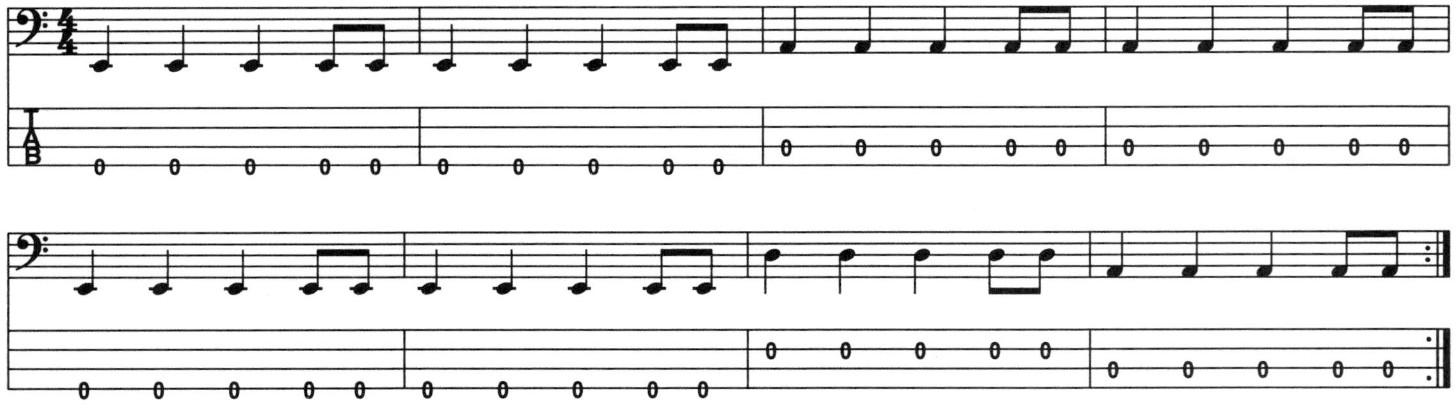

2.7 (B)

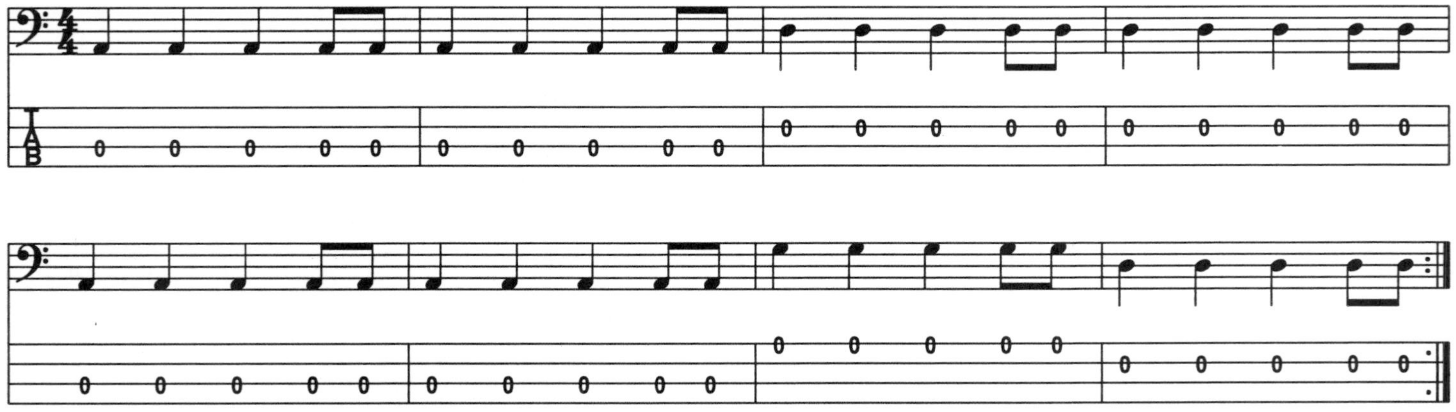

If you're ready to move on, let's go one step further and add sixteenth notes. Exercises 2.8 through 2.17 build upon the previous examples, and will help you gain precision, speed, dexterity, strength and stamina in the thumb.

Note the articulation markings on some of the sixteenth notes. The first one is played long and the second one short. Practice this articulation until you can play it correctly. In the following exercises, concentrate on precision of rhythm and attack.

2.8

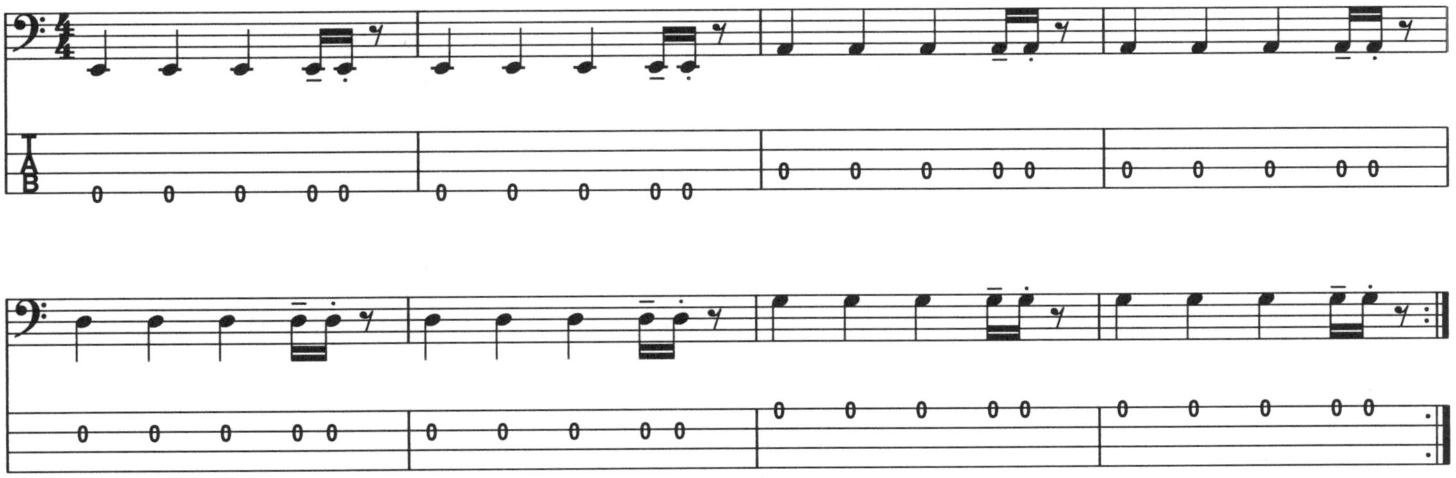

2.9

2.10

2.11

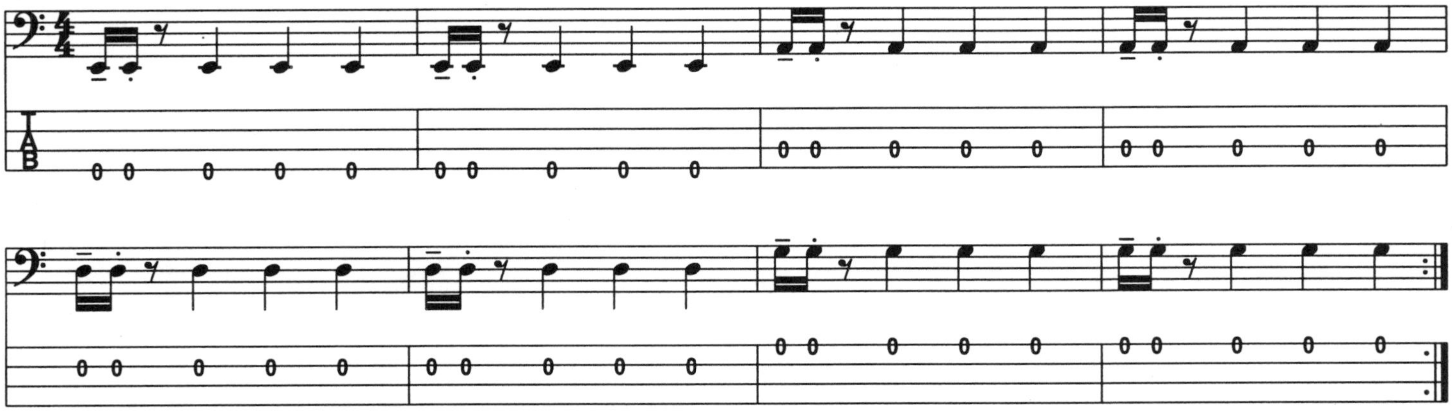

2.12

2.13

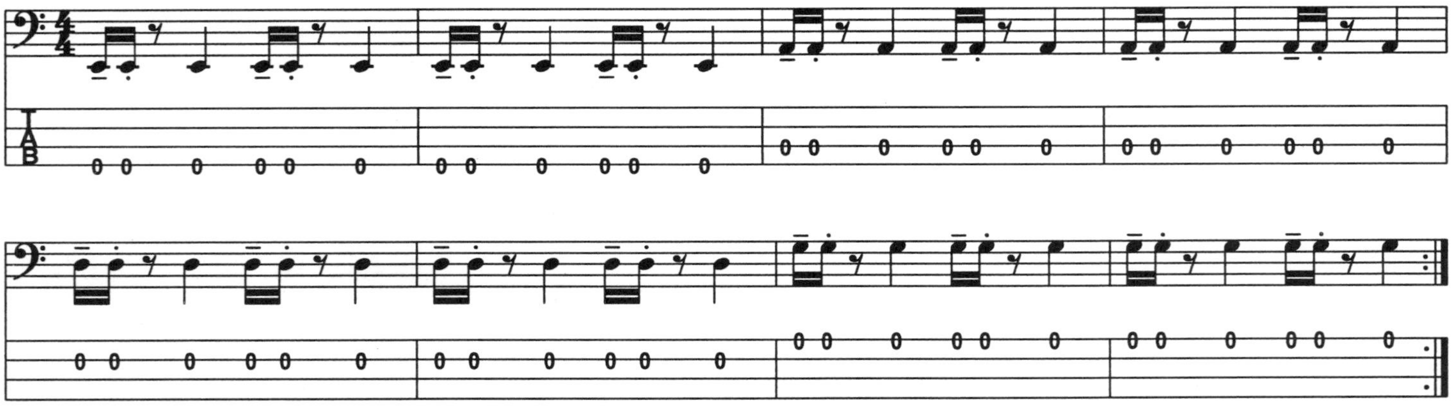

2.14

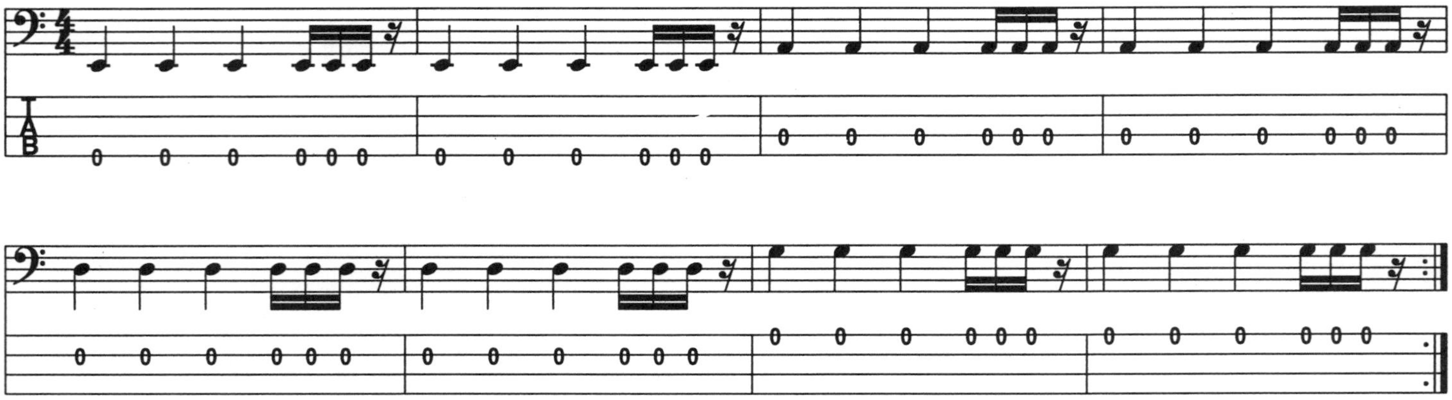

2.15

2.16

2.17

Now go back and practice Exercises 2.8 through 2.17 again, but instead of playing the "E" string first, the "A" string second, the "D" third and the "G" fourth, play them in the following sequences:

E-A-G-D	E-G-A-D	A-E-G-D
E-D-G-A	E-G-D-A	A-D-G-E
E-D-A-G	A-E-D-G	A-D-E-G

You can try starting on the "D" and the "G" strings, as well. These variations will help your string-crossing abilities. With any piece of music, the more ways you practice it and the more ways you find to look at it, the better you'll understand it, and the better you'll be able to play it.

Tired of open strings yet? Okay, let's give the left hand a little something to do. Play Exercise 2.18, using only the "E" and the "A" strings.

2.18

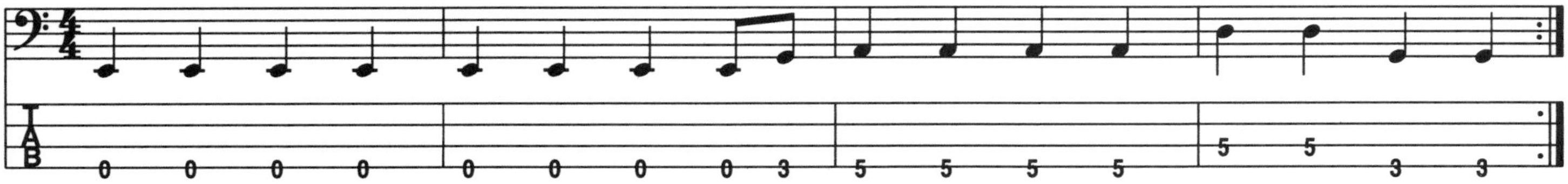

As you may have guessed, we'll vary these four bars in Exercises 2.19 through 2.21.

2.19

2.20

2.21

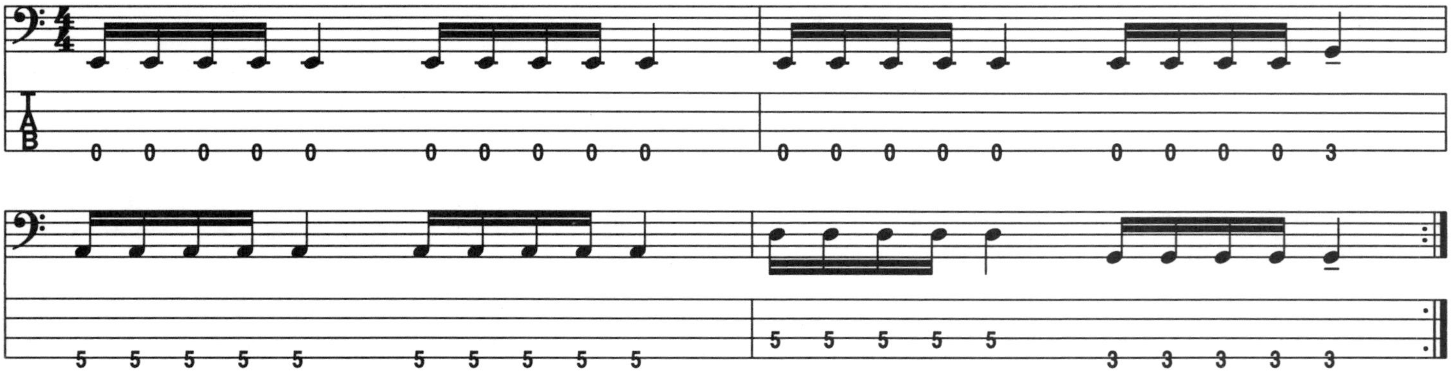

Now let's transfer what you've just done to the other strings.

2.22 (A)

2.22 (B)

2.23 (A)

2.23 (B)

2.24 (A)

2.24 (B)

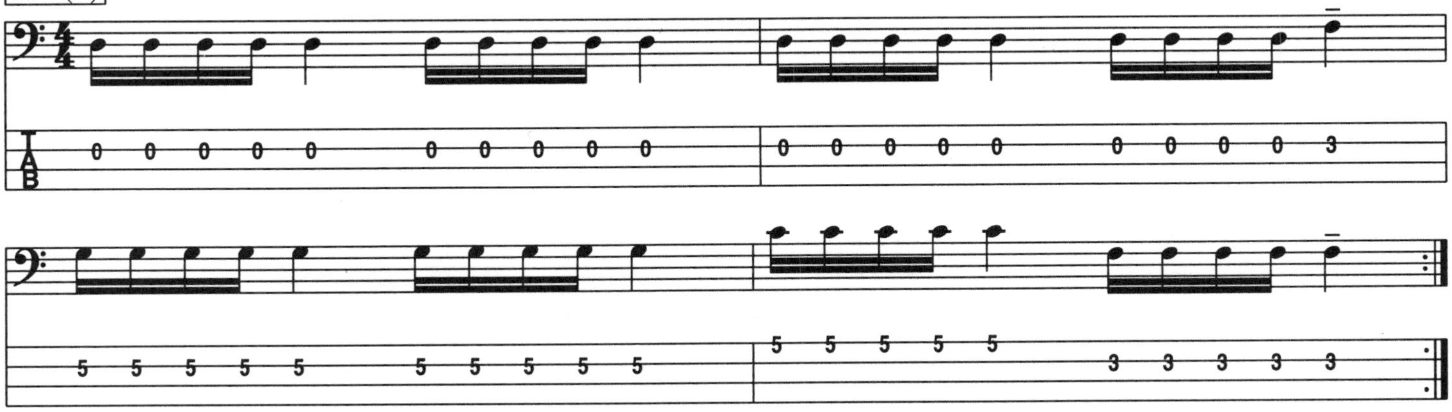

These exercises should give you a good command of the thumb technique. If you're comfortable with your slapping at this point, I'm ready to move on if you are.

The *Popping* Technique: "Popping" is the plucking, or "snapping" of the strings with one of the right-hand fingers. Most people use their index finger, though some prefer to pop with their middle finger. Some players alternate popping between their index and middle fingers, resulting in some pretty hip and scary stuff. Get the basic technique down and go as far as your creativity will take you.

Keep a couple things in mind while popping. First, instead of pressing the note all the way down on the fret, leave just a smidgen of "daylight" between the string and the fingerboard. This technique helps give the pop that percussiveness that typifies the funk sound. Make sure you push down hard enough to make the pitch recognizable. It'll take a little practice to find a comfortable balance.

Second, you've got to be very careful about extraneous noise, or "string-ring." This caution applies to all types of bass playing, but particularly to the funk style. With your hands in the slap/pop position, your strings are more vulnerable to this problem, so make sure you dampen them where necessary. Your tape recorder will help you tremendously with this matter.*

Popping the string with the 1st finger.

When playing funk bass, it is very common to slap on the downbeats and pop on the upbeats. In the following exercises, try to feel your metronome or drum machine playing the downbeats, while you supply the upbeats. Though these studies are simple, don't rush through them.

2.25

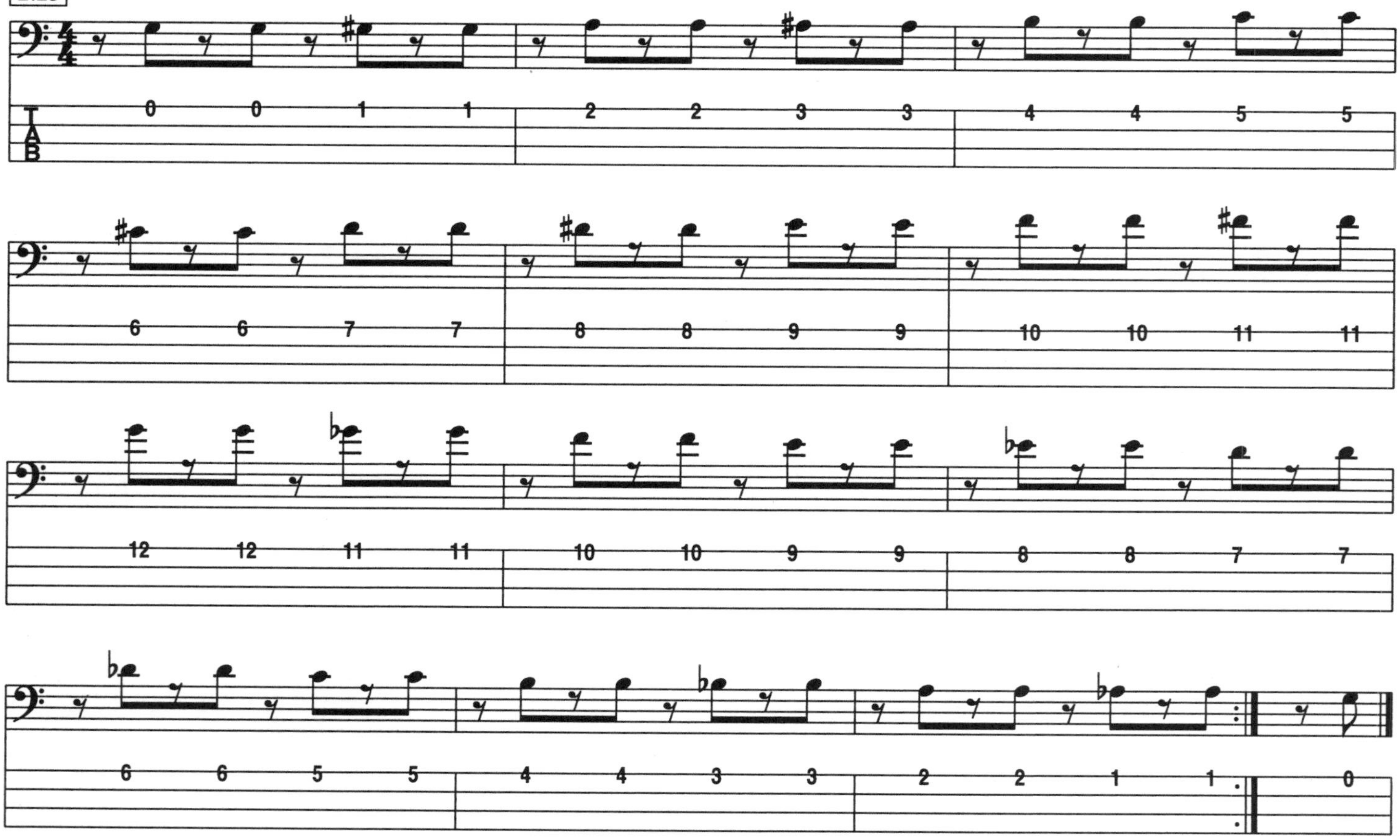

* The same caution about slapping in moderation applies to popping, as well, perhaps even more so. Please take it easy, at first. If you try too much today, you might not have much of a fingertip left tomorrow. By the way, how's that Charlie Parker solo coming along?

2.26

2.27

2.28

Review the exercises in this chapter. When you feel comfortable with basic slapping and popping, turn to Chapter 3 and we'll combine the two techniques into one cohesive style.

Just a reminder: *Everything in this book is important. Don't get too eager and skip to the end of the book without first learning the basics. All the exercises are presented in a logical, step-by-step order, so don't turn a page unless you're proficient in all the studies up to that point. Though some students may grasp certain concepts more quickly than others, I hope you'll at least read through all the exercises, without skipping anything. The biggest advantage to this gradual, one-step-at-a-time approach is that it gets better with every page!*

CHAPTER 3
SOME BASIC FUNK PATTERNS

Now that we're ready to combine the slapping and popping techniques, the most obvious way to begin is by playing octaves — the basic building blocks of many funk lines. In the following exercises, strive for precision and accuracy. Octave patterns seem simple to play, but the hard part is executing them *consistently, with a perfect time feel, for a long time!*

To make the downbeats sound like downbeats, and the upbeats, upbeats, slap a little harder (or in some cases, *a lot* harder) than you pop. That way, you'll sound more like you're grooving, rather than just floating.

Metronome markings have been deliberately omitted. The best way to "nail" these exercises is to start slowly, and increase the tempo gradually. See how long you can play these octave eighth notes without stopping.

3.1

3.2
T P T P T P T P
Simile

3.3

3.4

3.5

3.6

Now let's gradually start building some speed with the right thumb.

3.7

3.8
T P T T P T P T T P
Simile
TAB

3.3

3.4

3.11

T T P T T T P T T T P T T T P T
TAB
Simile

3.12

T T P T T T P T T T P T T T P T
TAB
Simile

3.13

3.14

Muted Notes. One of the characteristics that helps put the "funk" in funk bass is the use of muted notes, or notes of indefinite pitch. Following are variations on Exercises 3.7 through 3.14, utilizing muted notes.

The muted note technique is actually quite simple to achieve. Loosen up your left-hand* fingers until the pitch is not recognizable — just a ... well, just a ... *dead* note! This effect can be obtained while either slapping or popping. The goal is to achieve a more percussive sound. Be aware of where your hand is on the fingerboard. Make sure you aren't touching a harmonic, or else a note will ring, and the dead note will come to life! Also, in executing a muted note on an open string, you might need a little help from the "slapping-hand" wrist in order to keep the string from vibrating. This technique takes a little practice. Start slowly.

*"Fingerboard-hand," okay, lefties?

3.15

3.16

3.17
T P T T P T P T T P
Simile
3.18
T P T T P T P T T P
Simile

3.19

3.20

3.21

3.22

Once you're at ease with these exercises, try to really build up the tempos. They sound best when played very fast, and are a lot of fun, too.

Now let's try triplets.

3.23

3.24

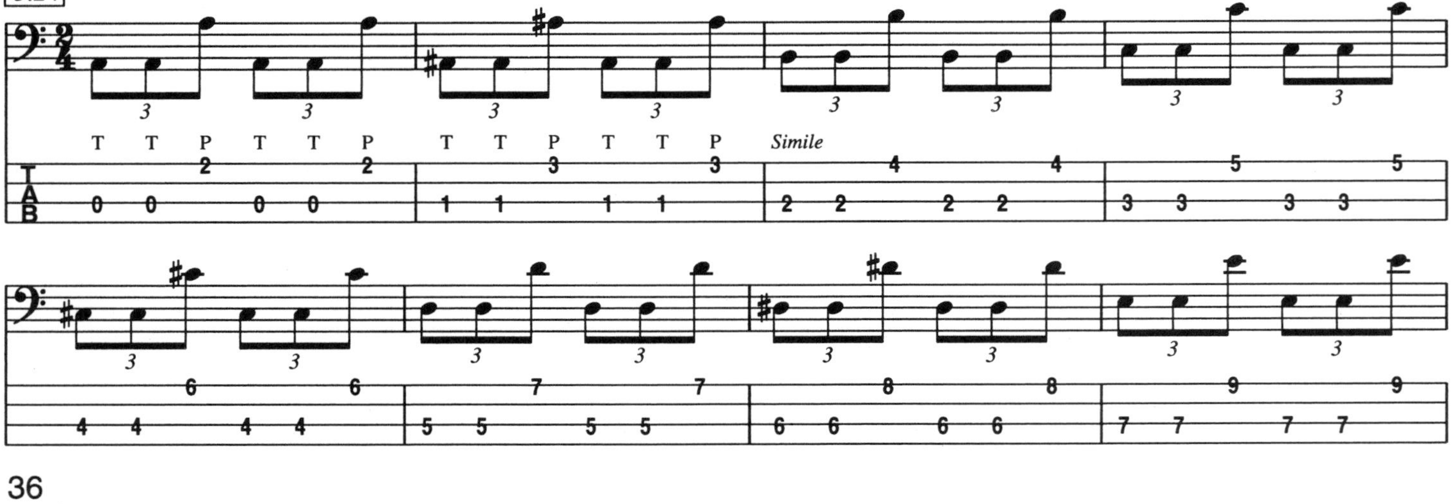

3.25
T T P T T P T T P T T P
Simile
TAB

3.26

3.27

3.28
T P T T P T
Simile

3.29

3.30

And triplets with muted notes:

3.32
T T P T T P
Simile

3.33

3.34

3.35
T P T T P T
Simile

3.36
T P T T P T
Simile

3.37

3.38

The next group of exercises builds upon the previous studies. It includes variations of eighth- and sixteenth-notes and triplets, with and without muted notes. Spend some time on these studies, and make sure you play them properly and cleanly. They will help you build technique and endurance.

3.39 (A)

3.39 (B)

3.40

3.41 (A)

3.41 (B)

3.42

3.43 (A)

3.43 (B)

3.44

3.45 (A)

3.45 (B)

3.46

3.47 (A)

3.47 (B)

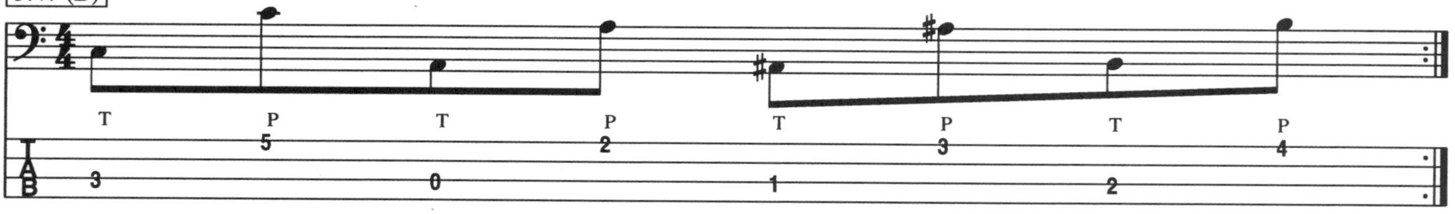

3.48 (A)

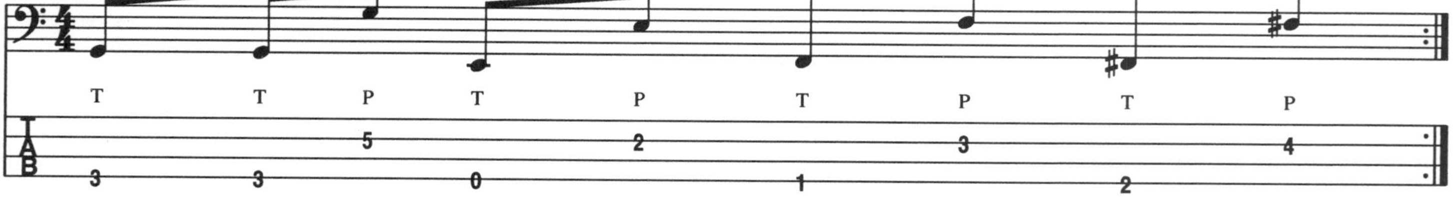

3.48 (B)

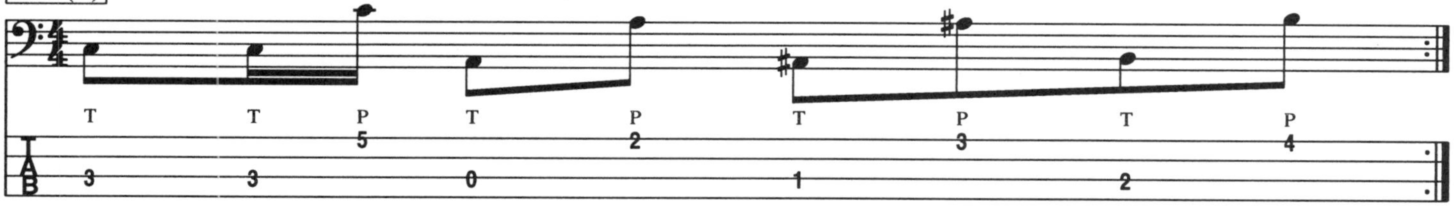

3.49 (A)

3.49 (B)

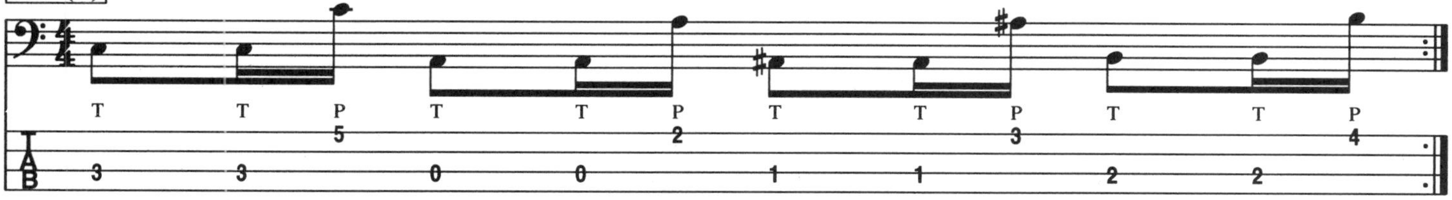

3.50 (A)

3.50 (B)

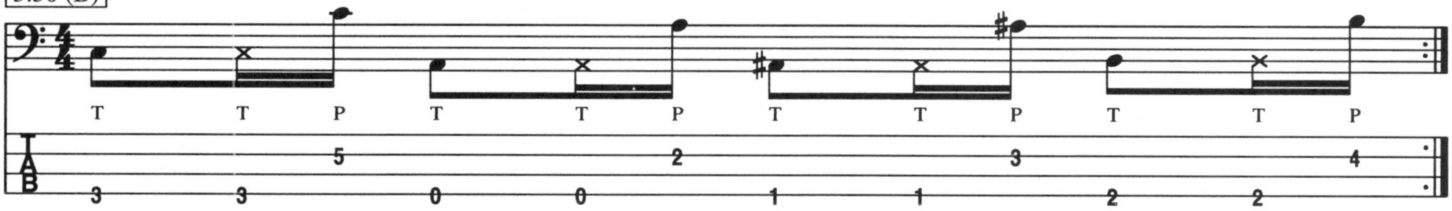

3.51 (A)

3.51 (B)

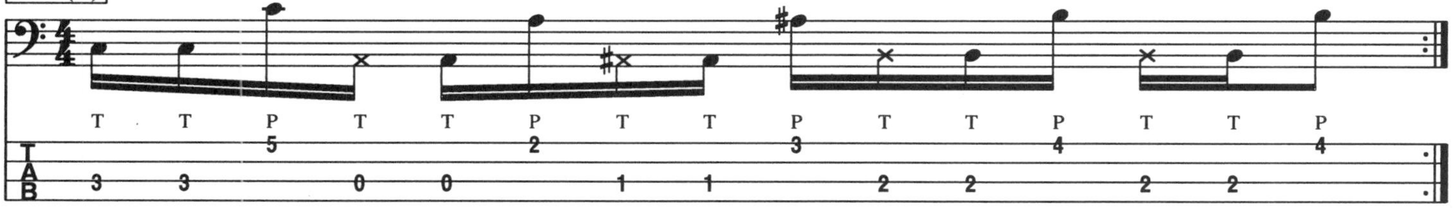

This next exercise, sort of a 16-bar blues, is still on the technical side, but it sounds musical, nonetheless. See how fast you can play this one, and how long you can keep it up. It's fun.

3.52

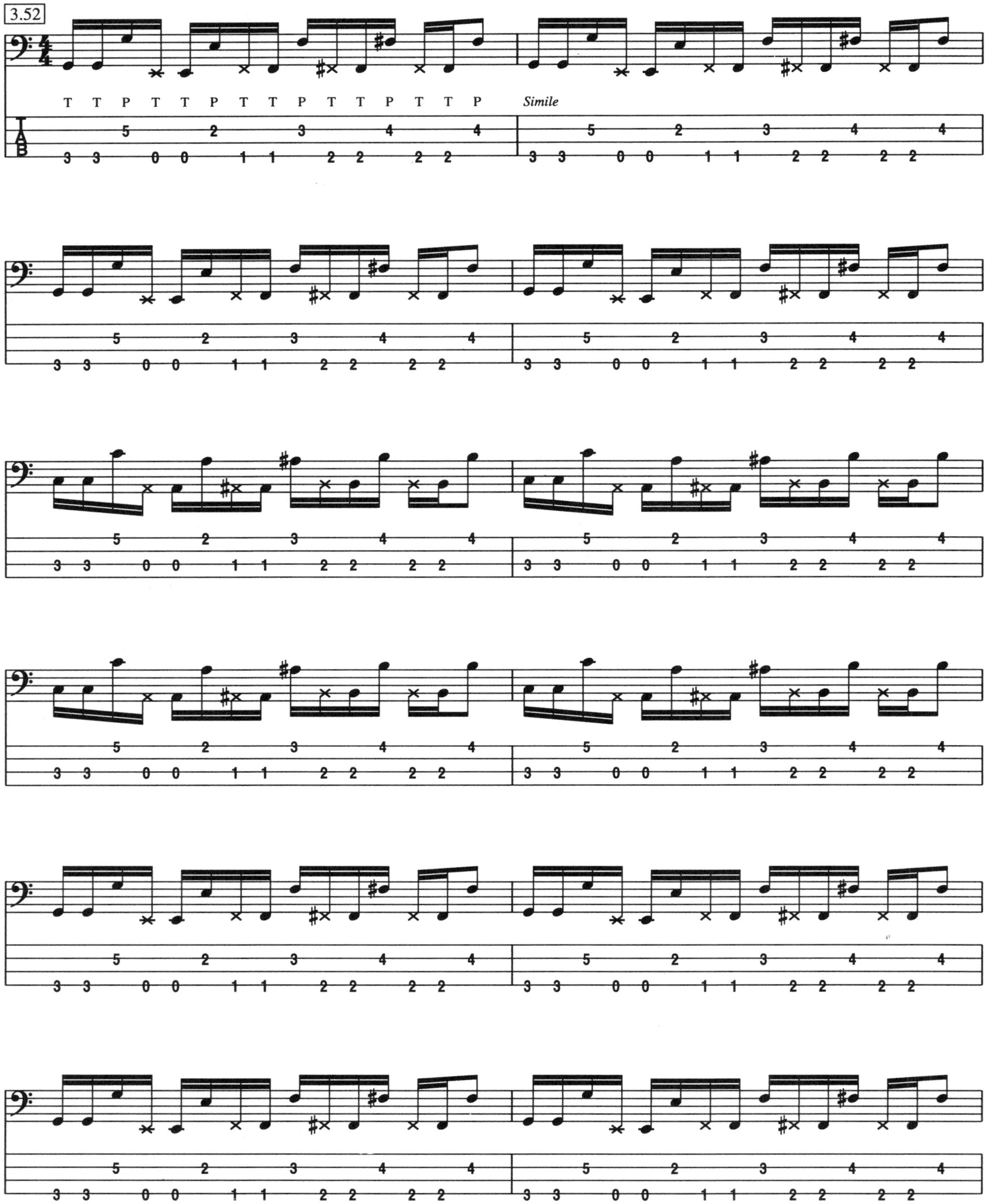

Reminder: *In addition to playing correctly, an important part of your job is to play consistently for indefinite lengths of time. During a live performance, a million different "hungry" soloists may share the limelight, one after another. If that's the case, a good bass player is expected to be solid and right on the money, and can't afford to lose the beat, not even for a second! It would be a good idea to refer to this chapter often, since it's fundamental by nature, and could also serve as a good warm-up. You may even want to log in your practice book how long you were able to sustain a single pattern, and at what tempo. This kind of practice will take some discipline, but it's crucial. Use your tape recorder. Use your drum machine. Do it!*

Chapter 4
Style Elements

Before we go much further, we ought to talk about a few basic elements of style. You're probably familiar with some or all of these techniques, but let's make sure we're playing them correctly and accurately.

The *Hammer-on.* A *hammer-on* produces a note by slamming a finger onto the fingerboard as opposed to actually picking the string. In most cases a previous note has been struck and is still ringing on the same string, adding momentum to the hammer-on. However, it is also possible for a note to be produced by the *hammer-on* technique itself. This technique provides variety in your articulation, and also allows you to play faster by relieving the right hand of some of the work. To play the *hammer-ons* in Exercise 4.1, slap the first note with the thumb and articulate the second note by "hammering" a left-hand finger down on the string with enough force to sound the note.

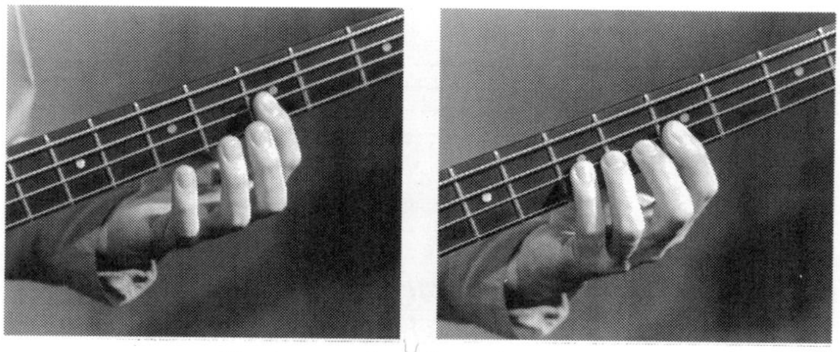

Hammer-on from 1st to 4th finger.

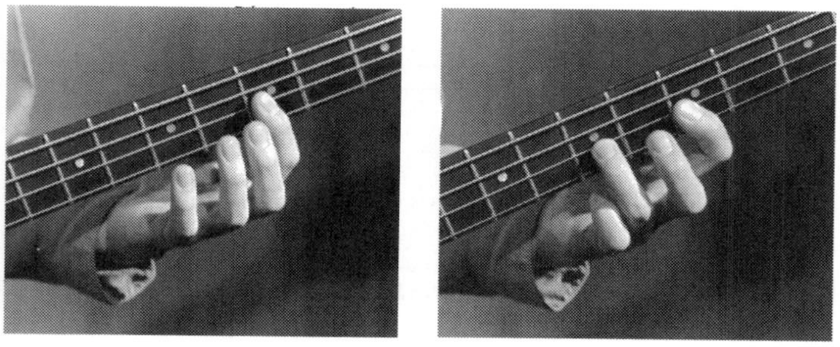

Hammer-on from 1st to 3rd finger.

4.1

Now let's try it on the other strings.

4.2

4.3

Exercises 4.4 through 4.12 are a bit more challenging. Actually, *hammer-ons* are pretty easy to play, so you shouldn't have too much trouble. Just start slowly.

4.4

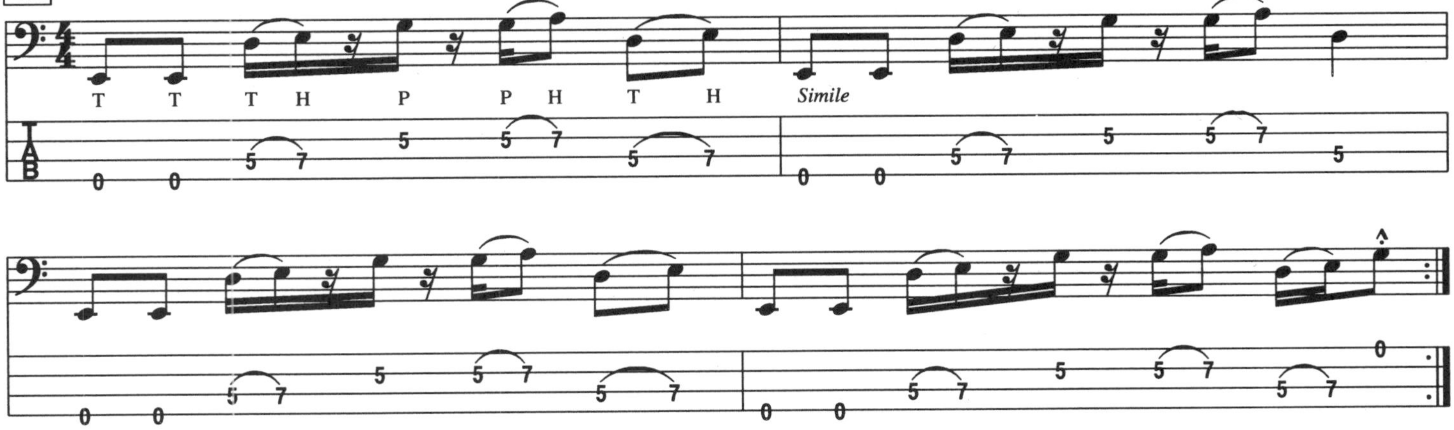

4.5

4.6

4.7

4.8

4.9

4.10

4.11

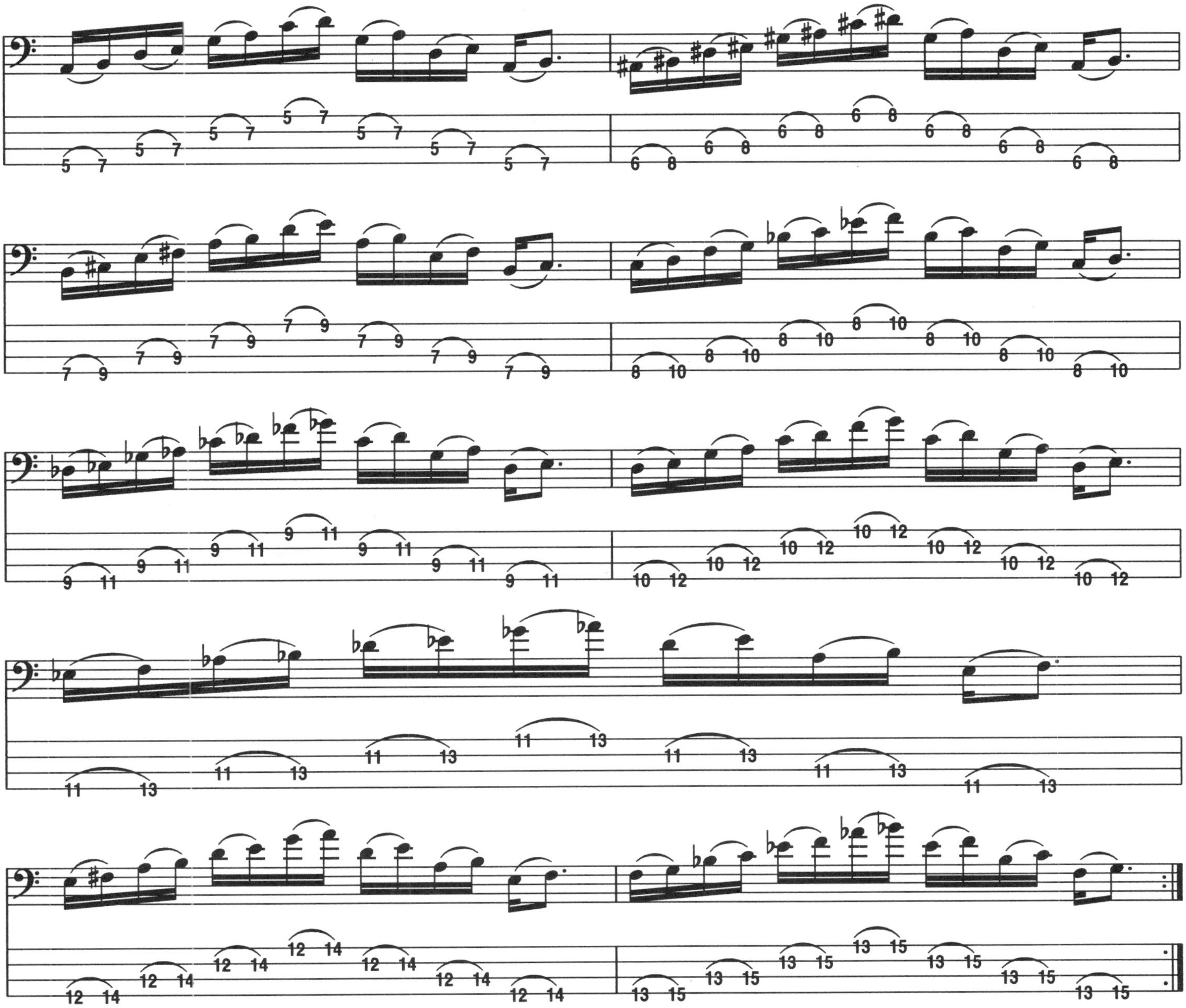

4.12

The *Pull-off.* A very close relative of the *hammer-on* , the *pull-off* is another variation in articulation, or another "trick." A bit more difficult than the *hammer-on*, the *pull-off* is executed by a left-hand finger pulling *off* the string, with a sort of downward "flicking" motion. Before you pull, you must have a note pressed down on another fret, ready to "take over." The most common pair of left-hand fingers used in a *pull-off* is the "ring-to-index" combination, but any other pattern is possible.

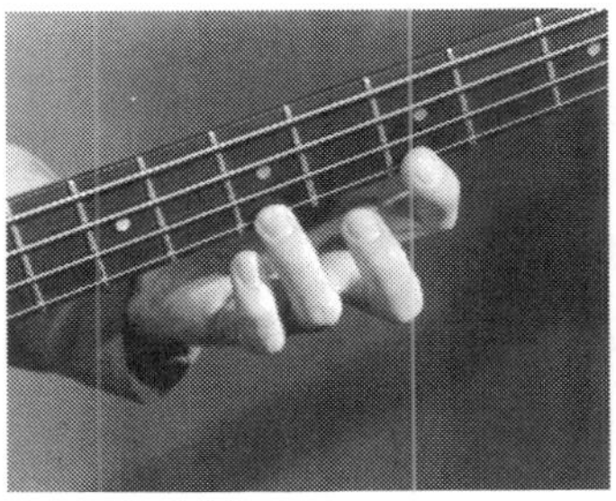

3rd finger *pull-off* to 1st finger

2nd finger *pull-off* to 1st finger

Try these exercises.

4.13

4.14

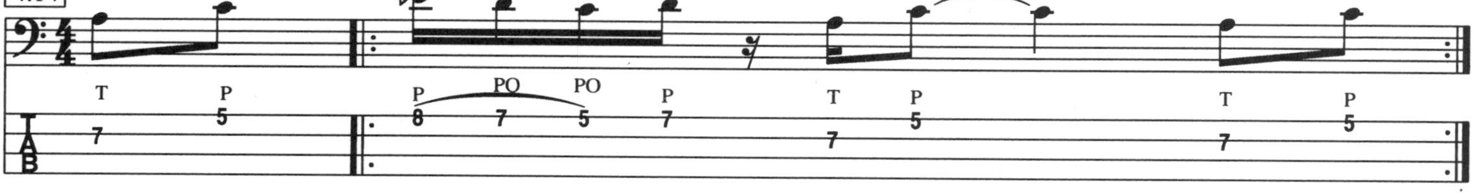

4.15

4.16

4.17

The *Slide*. Sometimes you want to move from one fret to another, but you don't want to "lift a finger." Enter the *slide*. Make sure your finger is pushed all the way down on the fingerboard while sliding between notes. Sliding will make your playing more legato (smooth). It can add personality, as well. Slide around on these a little:

4.18

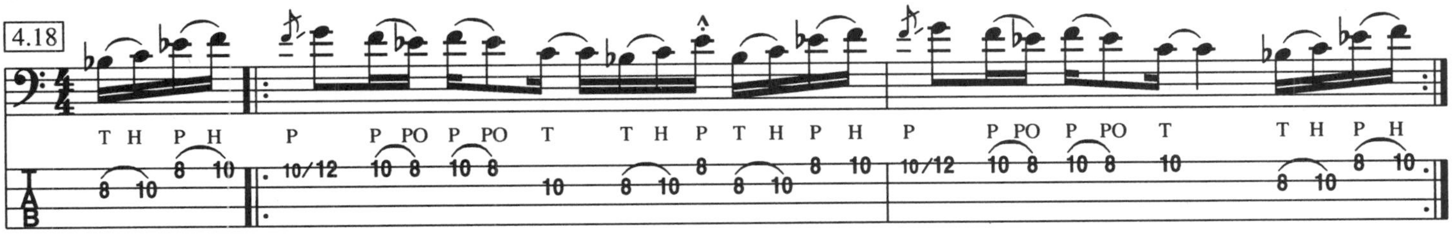

4.19

The *Trill*. The *trill* is a fast *hammer-on/pull-off* combination that keeps repeating itself. Theoretically, there are six fingering possibilities:* "index-to-middle," "index-to-ring," "index-to-pinky," "middle-to-ring," "middle-to-pinky" and "ring-to-pinky." As you build your technique and strengthen your fingers, you may want to use any or all finger combinations. The strongest combinations are "index-to-middle" and "index-to-ring," but, hey, anything's possible. See how many ways you can finger these exercises:

The *Trill*

4.20

4.21

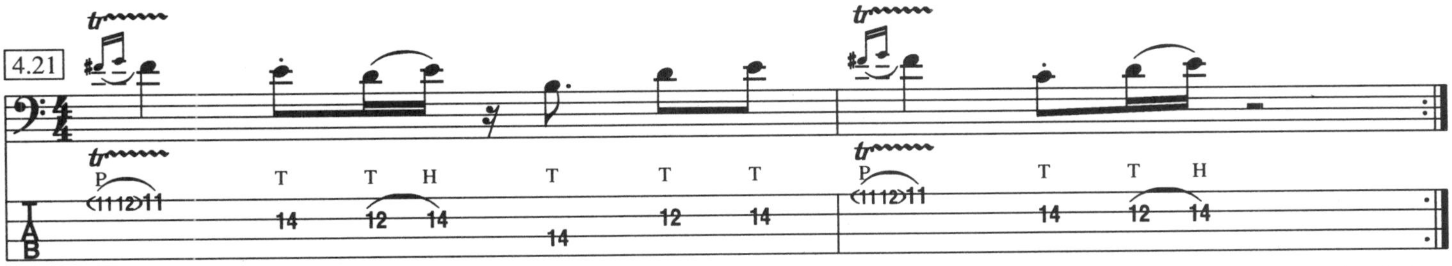

4.22

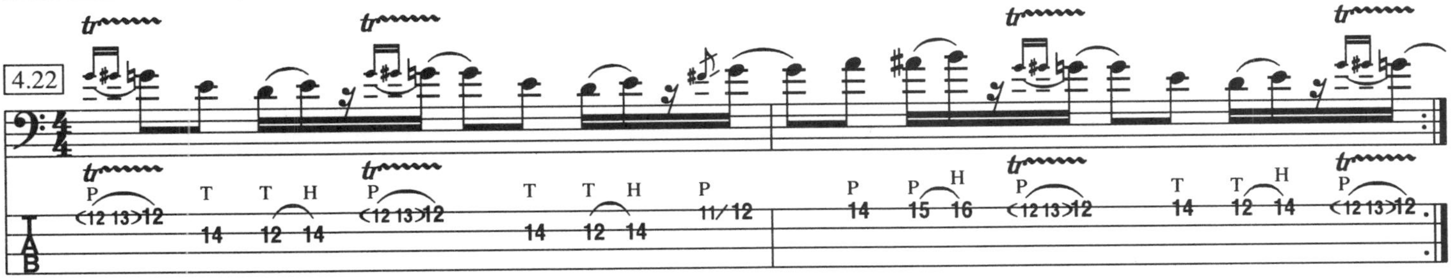

* With tapping techniques, the use of the thumb (or thumbs), and a little creativity, the possibililities are limitless. For now, let's just say there are six basic fingerings.

4.23

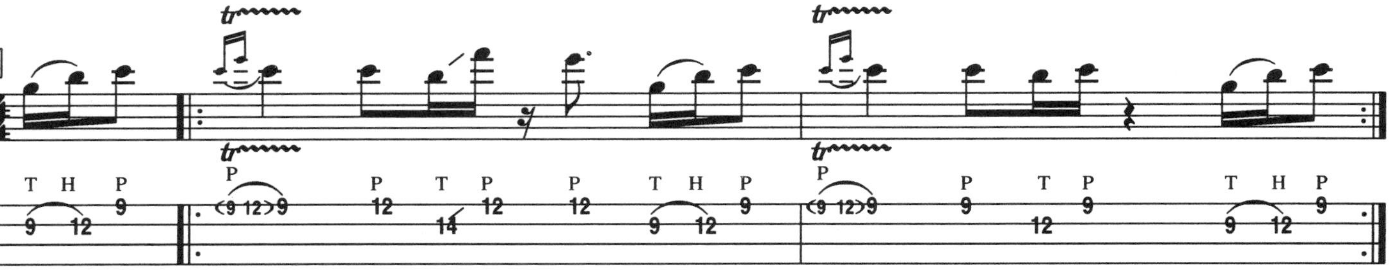

4.24

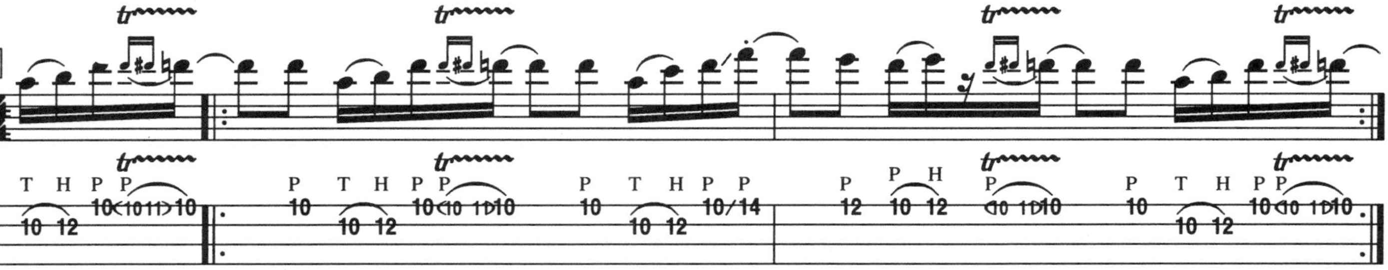

The *Shake*. This one's important to master. Once you get it down and sounding right and throw it in in just the right place, your funk will get funkier and heavier. Somewhat similar to the *trill*, the *shake* is a fast alternating of two notes on a single string. The difference is that the *shake* uses only one finger, sliding back and forth. Use any finger you want. Don't underestimate the pinky, here. Often it's my favorite choice.

One thing to keep in mind about the *shake* as it relates to funk bass: generally speaking, wherever a *trill* sounds hip, a *shake* will sound hipper.

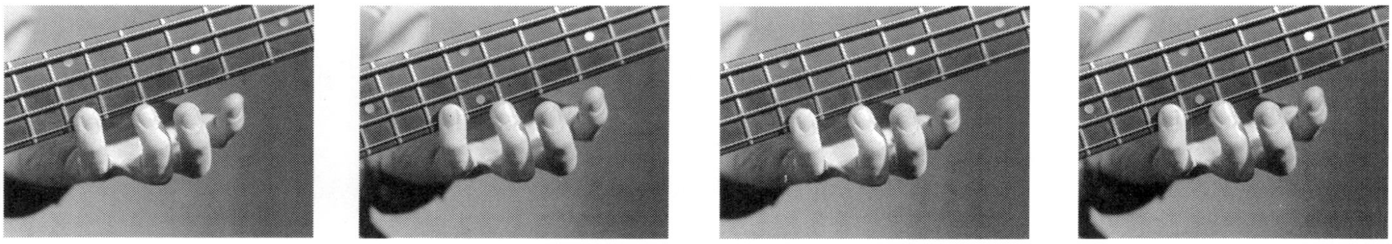

The *Shake*: Finger alternates between two adjacent frets.

4.25

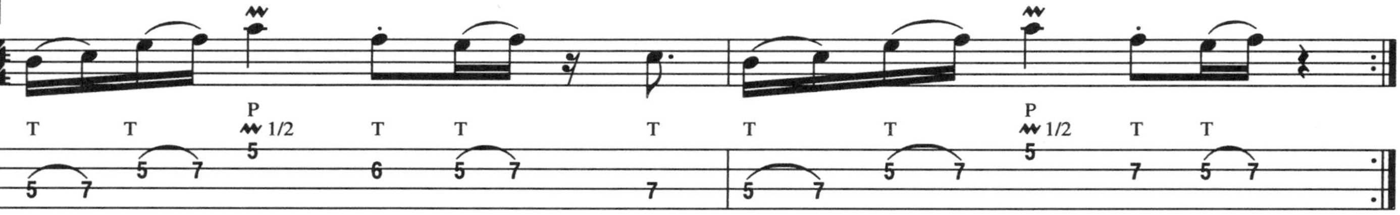

4.26

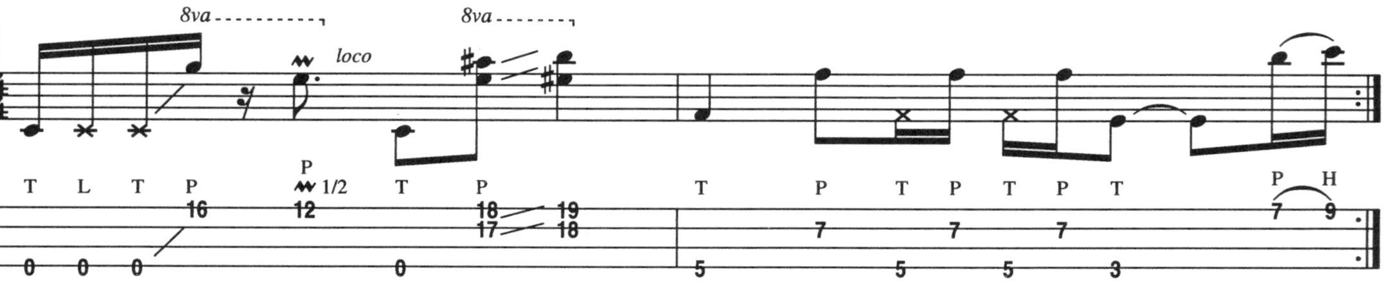

4.27

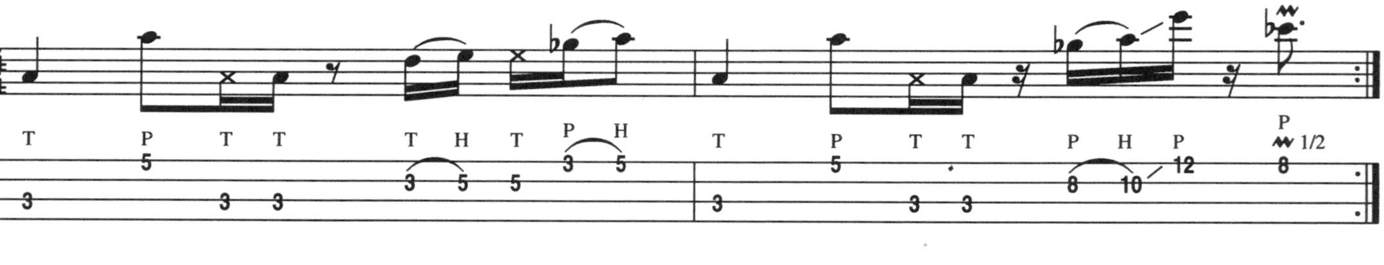

4.28

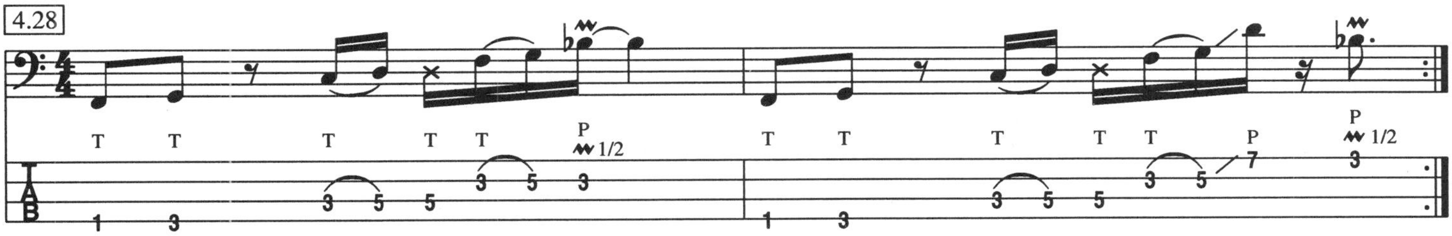

The *Bend*. I guess we got this one from the guitar players. Bending the string up or down, without moving your finger to another fret, will raise the pitch. The amount the pitch is raised depends, of course, on how much you bend the string. Bends can sound pretty corny if you don't play them properly. Use this technique sparingly. Try these exercises:

The *Bend*

4.29

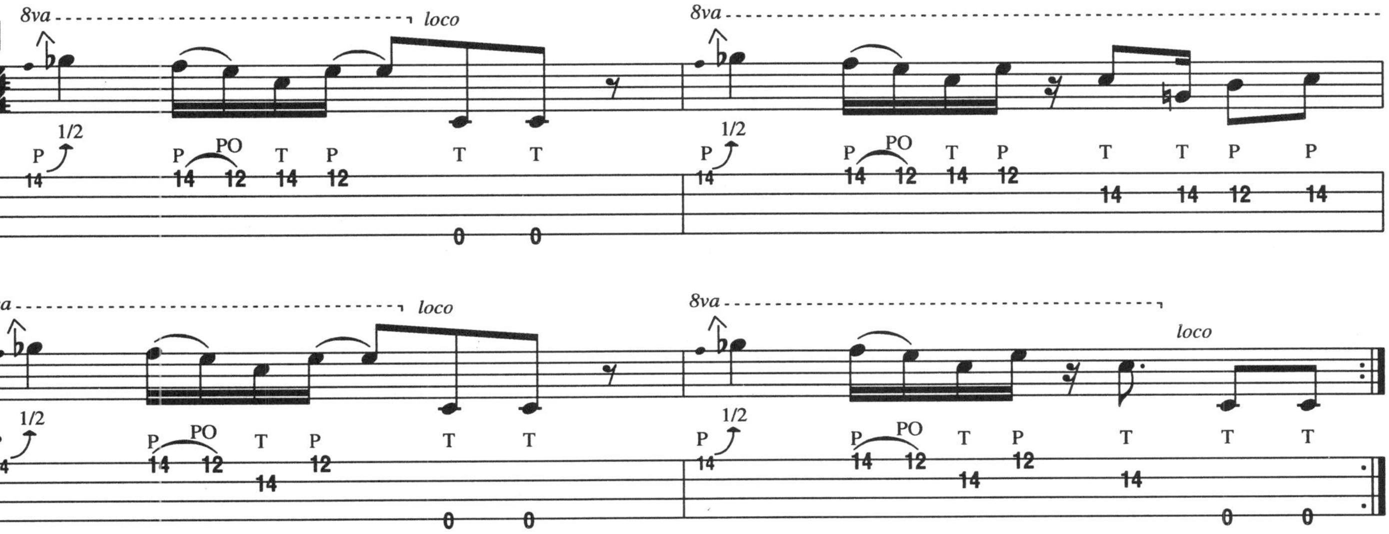

4.30

Keep working with these techniques until you're comfortable with them. They'll start to make a lot more sense when we combine them with grooves and licks. Your tape recorder will be a big help here. When you're ready, let's funk on!

CHAPTER 5
ESTABLISHING A GROOVE

Many of the exercises in this chapter are, musically speaking, the simplest in the book. **THAT'S THE POINT**. Remember, your job as a bass player is to "lay it down" and in almost every case, KEEP IT SIMPLE. The bass, by nature, is a supportive instrument. We bass players often have to play repetitive figures over and over again with little (or sometimes no) variation. This kind of playing takes some discipline, but it's this repetitiveness of the bass figure, along with the drums, that holds the music together and creates what we've all come to know as a *groove.* It's this ability to groove and to lock in with the drummer that distinguishes a good bass player from one who plays too much, or inappropriately.

As always, a metronome is crucial, but as we get more into grooving, a drum machine will make your music *feel* better and more fun to play. In many cases, just hearing the sound of the bass drum on "one" and "three," with a heavy back beat from the snare drum on "two" and "four," is enough to make all the difference in the world (or better yet, have the bass drum play "one" the upbeat of "two," and the downbeat of "three," with the snare on "two" and "four"). Of course, if you have a "real live" drummer to play with that's even better. Use your tape recorder to judge how well you're "locking in."

Which brings us to another important point. Locking in, though nobody said it was simple, is more complicated than it seems. Do you need to play *on top* of the beat (pushing the time, but not rushing)? Do you need to play a little *behind* the beat (pulling back, but not dragging)? Or do you need to play "right in the pocket?" A bass player and a drummer can be "great" musicians, but they won't sound good together unless they agree, not only on where to put the beat, but where to play *within* the beat. The answer, like anything else, comes from experience. Experience comes from listening and playing (repeat as necessary).

Another important consideration is the tempo at which you are playing. Everybody wants to play fast. That's fine. It's just as important, though, to groove at 60 and 80 beats per minute as it is at 200. What's more, it's *harder* to groove at slower tempos, so make sure you don't neglect them.* Keep asking yourself, "Am I really grooving?"

Once you feel competent with your groove playing, you'll want to insert some fills. The trick is knowing what to play and when. A mature player knows when to add a fill, what kind, and how long, and then gets right back to the business of laying down time. We'll get more into this concept in Chapter 6. In the meantime, just play what's written, let the music breathe and keep it simple!

5.1

5.2

*Actually, a slow groove usually sounds "groovier" than a fast groove, if it's played soulfully. There's a certain dirty, *nasty* element that just can't be captured at 300 beats per minute, but it's the funkiest thing in the world at 60 or 80.

5.3

5.4

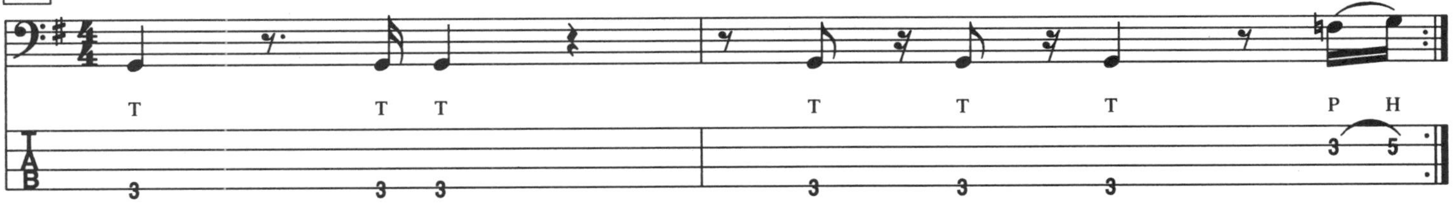

5.5

5.6

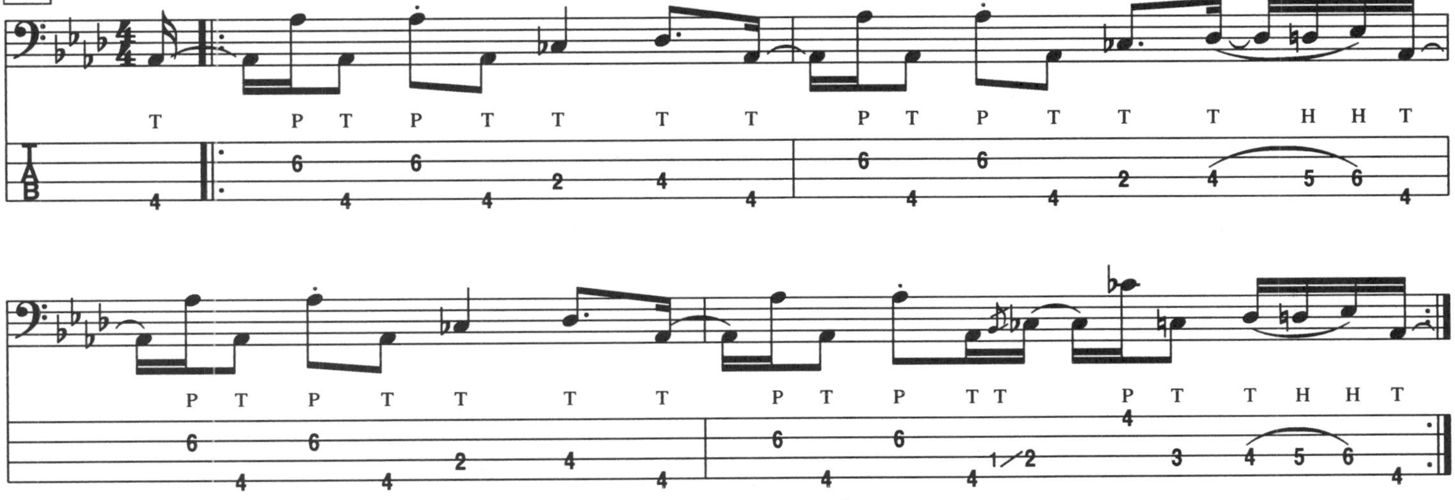

5.7

5.8

5.9

5.10

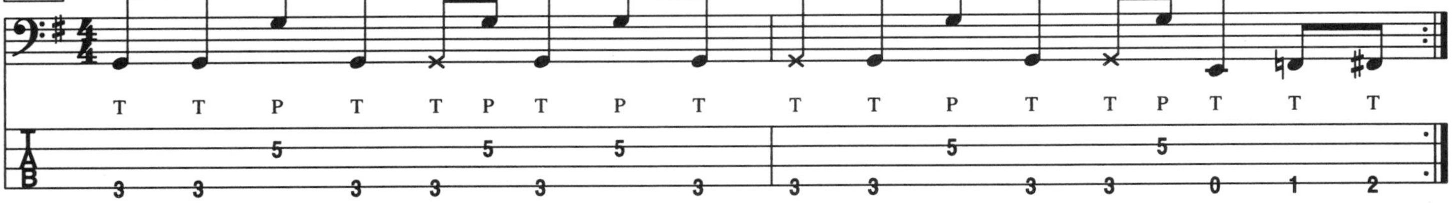

5.11

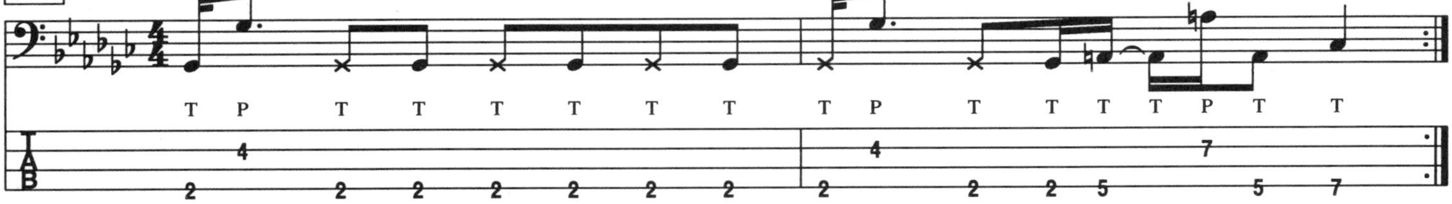

5.12

5.13

5.14
5.15
5.16
5.17
5.18

5.19

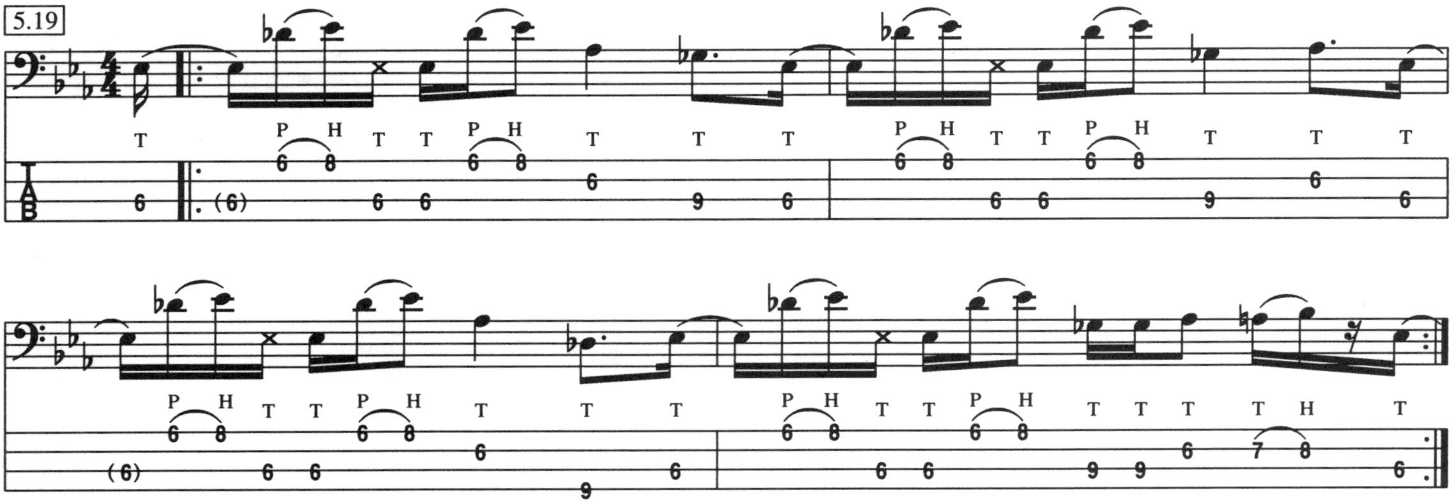

5.20

5.21

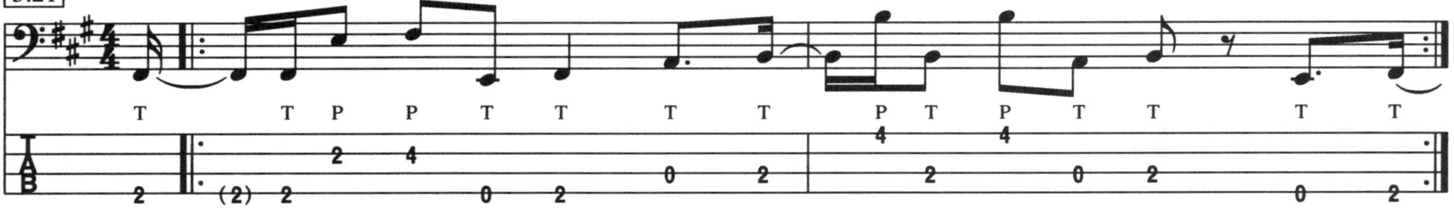

5.22

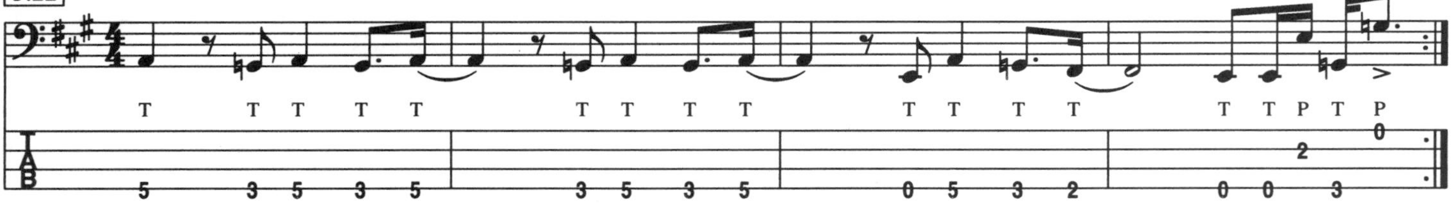

5.23

5.24

5.25

5.26

5.27

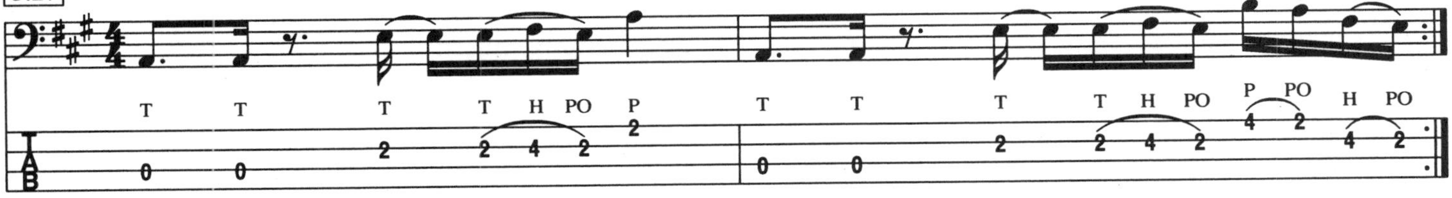

5.28

5.29

5.30

5.31

5.32

5.33

5.34

5.35

5.36

5.37

5.38

5.39

5.40

5.41

5.42

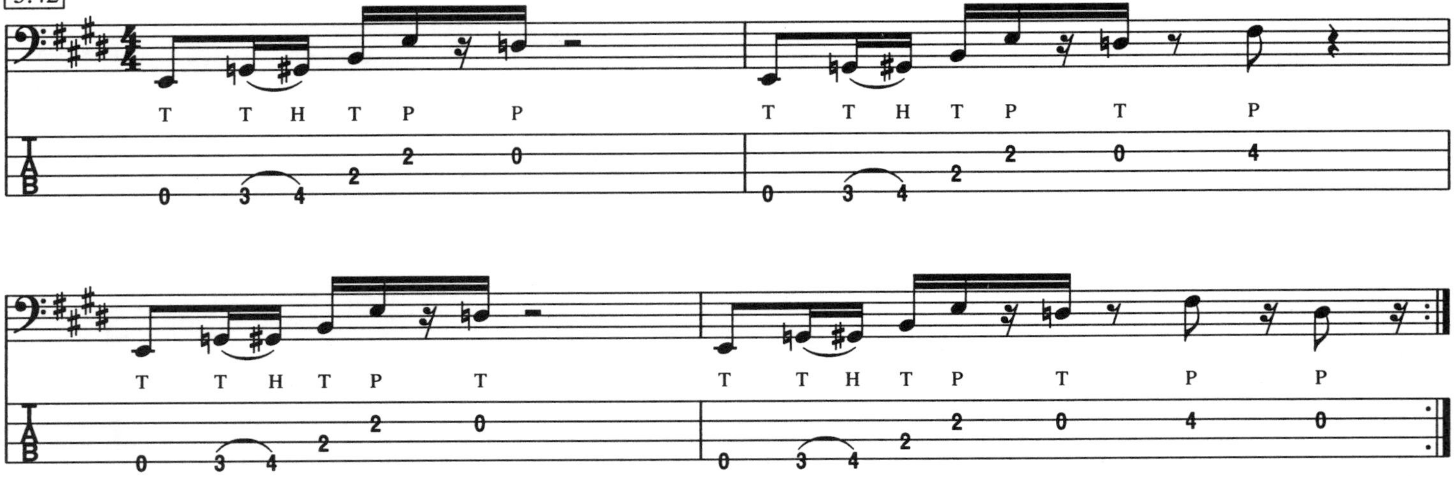

5.43

5.44

5.45

5.46

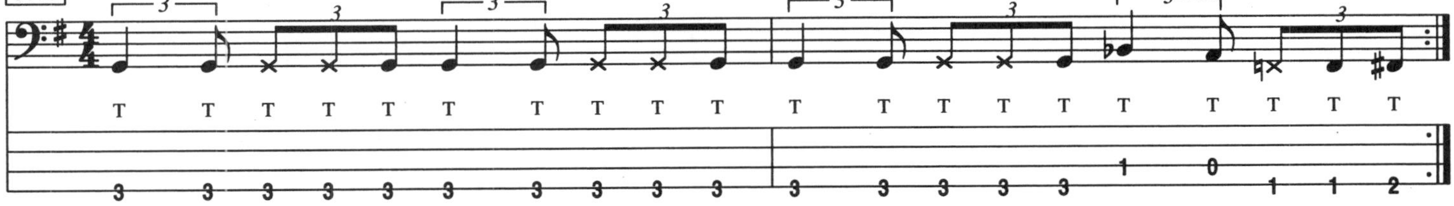

5.47

5.48

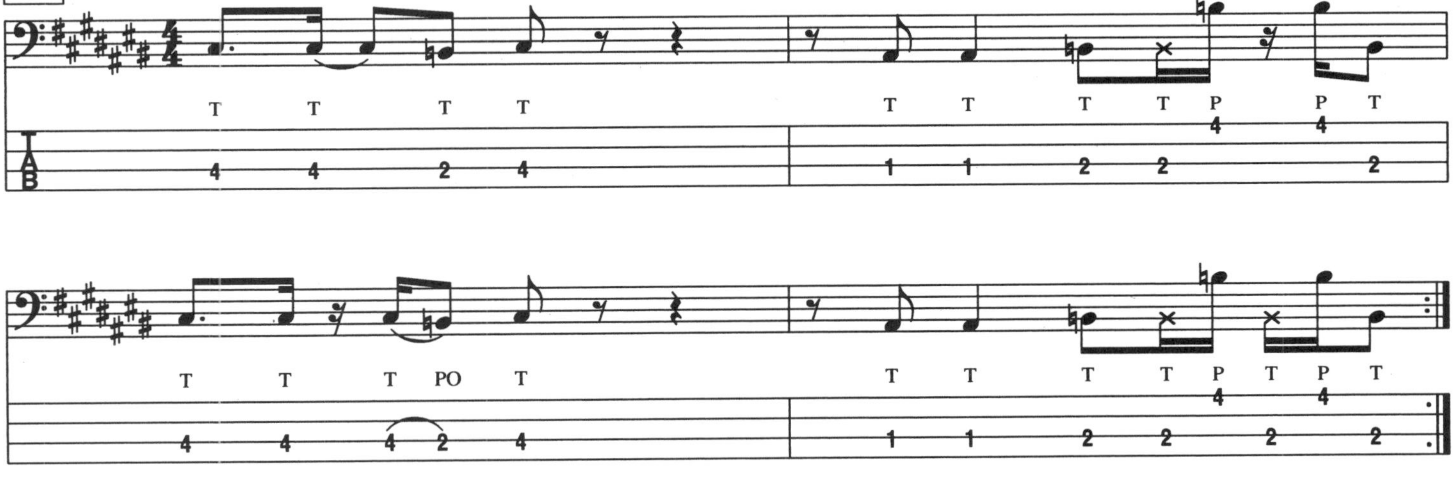

5.49

5.50

5.51

5.52

5.53

5.54

5.55

5.56

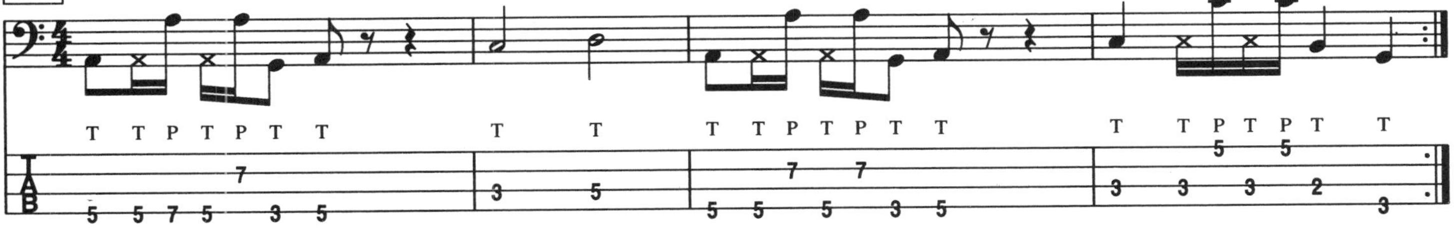

5.57

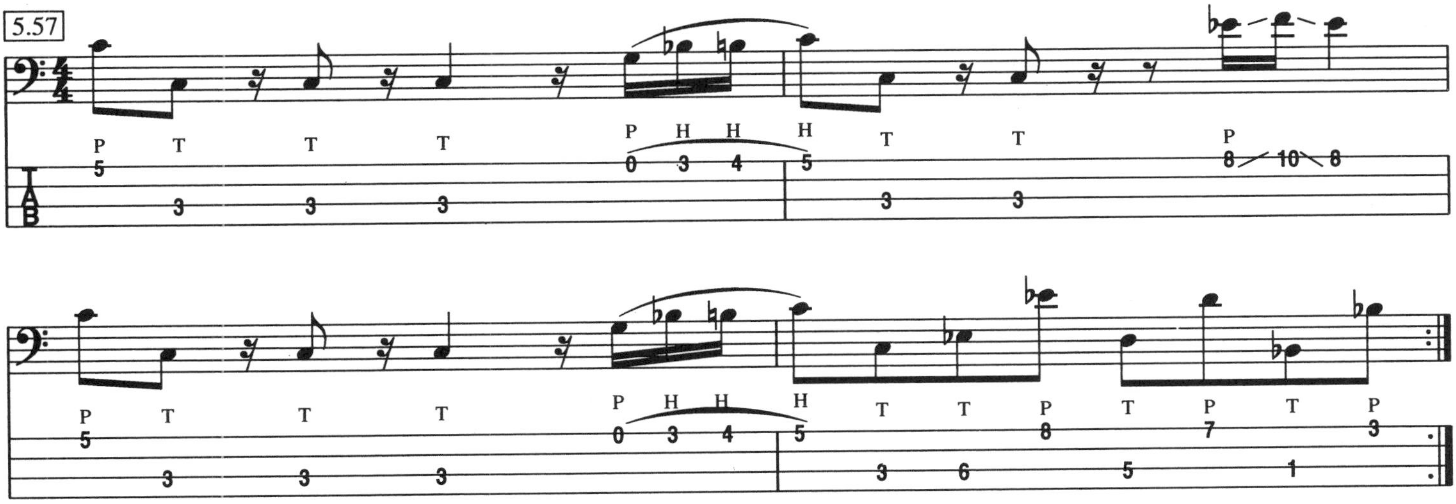

5.58

5.59

5.60

5.61

Chapter 6
Building A Vocabulary For Funk Soloing

This chapter was the most fun, and the most difficult to write. Fun, because it contains all the *pizazz* that we bassists like to use to show off during our solos. Difficult, because I had to slow everything down to dissect all these licks and analyze exactly what I was doing in order to make my bass sound funky. Notating it was tedious, but also quite fun and enlightening (now I know what I've been doing all these years!).

Your job is to make musical sense of all this. The tape will be a big help here. Your goal should be to get so comfortable with these pages that you can play them instinctively. The ultimate goal is to understand the groove concept and be able to handle a funk situation all by yourself, without the aid of a book.

Take your time with these licks. Eventually, you'll be able to get loose and feel them rather than read them. Remember, only play these types of licks when appropriate (i.e., during fills and solos), and don't try to steal the spotlight all the time. Following this advice will make you a more popular funk bassist. Trust me.

6.1

6.2

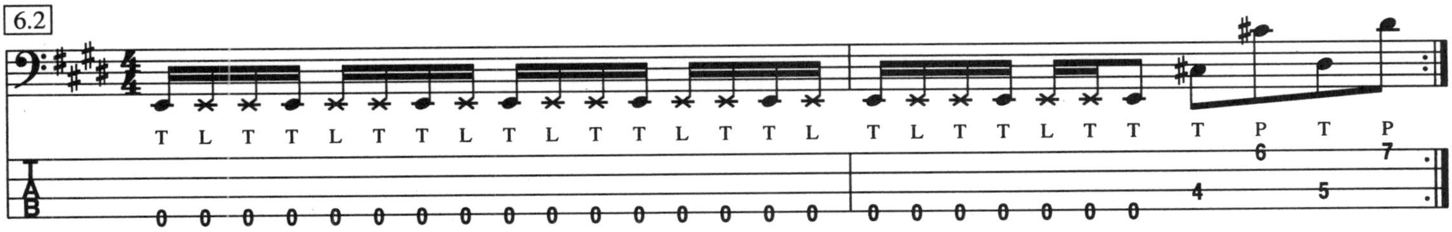

6.3

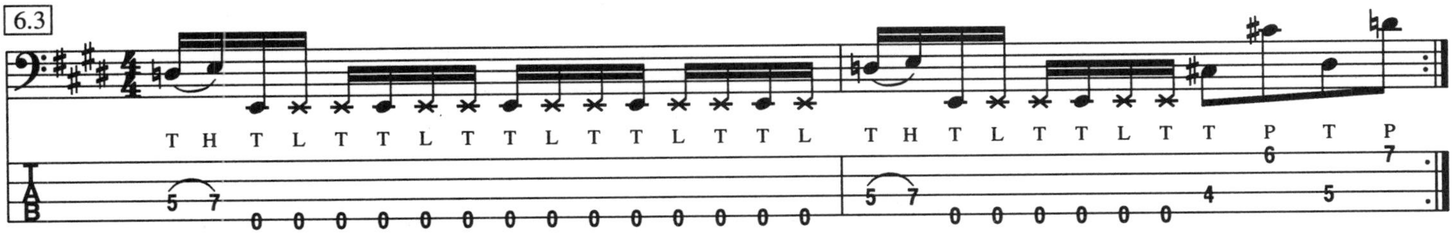

6.4

6.5

6.6

6.7

6.8

6.9

6.10

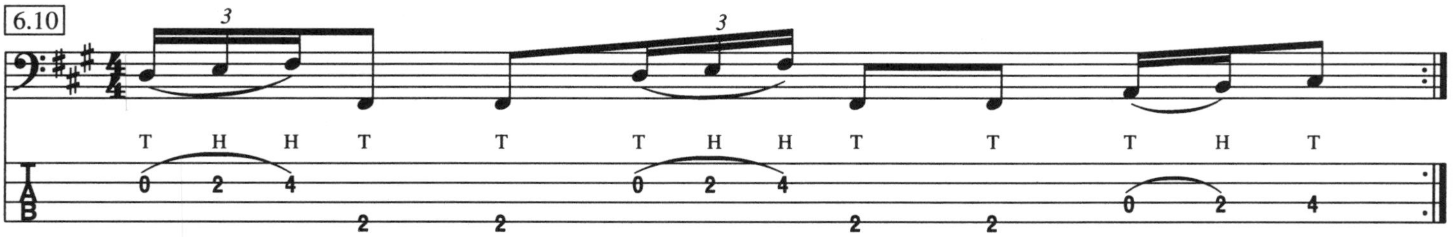

6.11

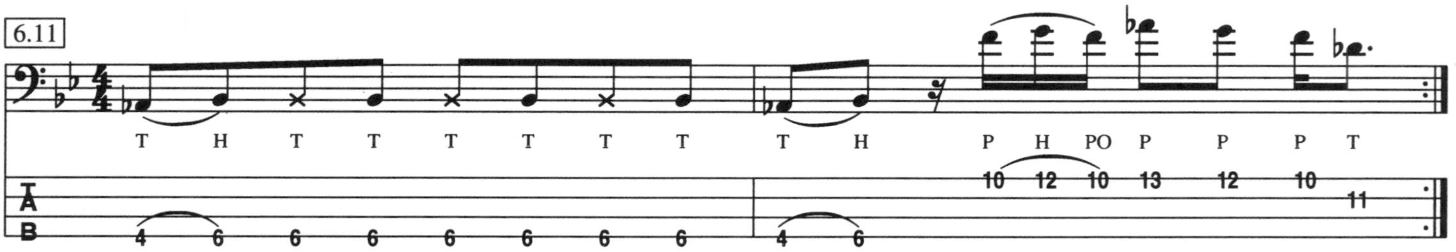

6.12
6.13
6.14
6.15
6.16

6.17

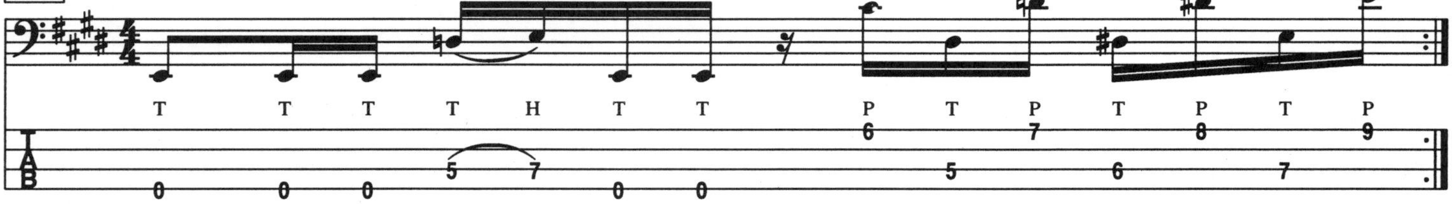

6.18

6.19

6.20

6.21

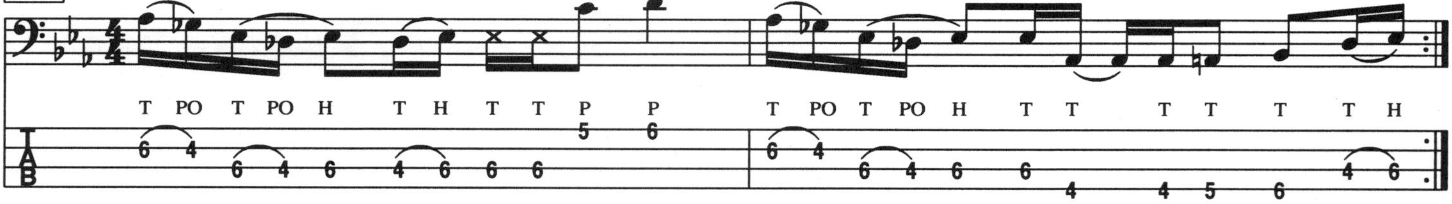

6.22

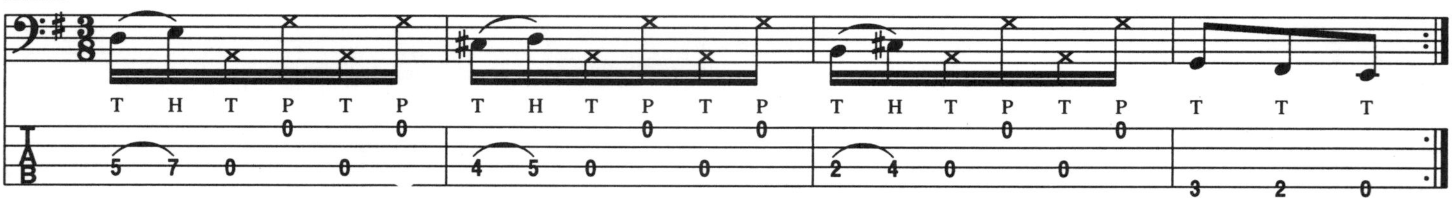

6.23

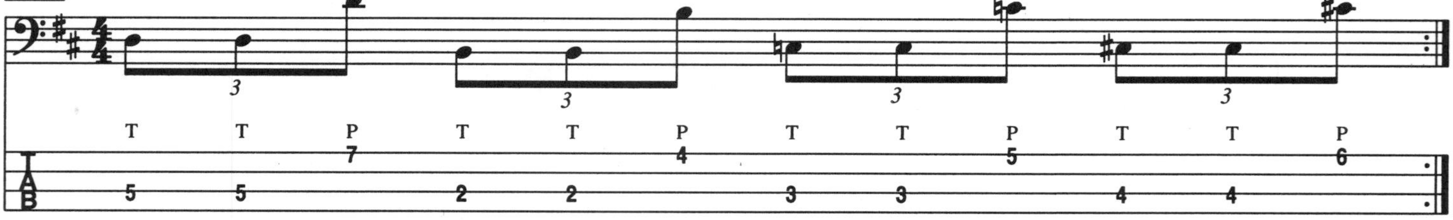

6.24

6.25

6.26

6.27

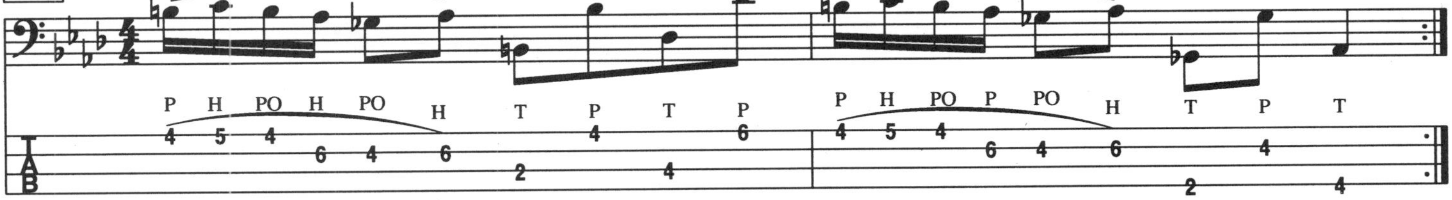

6.28

6.29

6.30

6.31

6.32

6.33

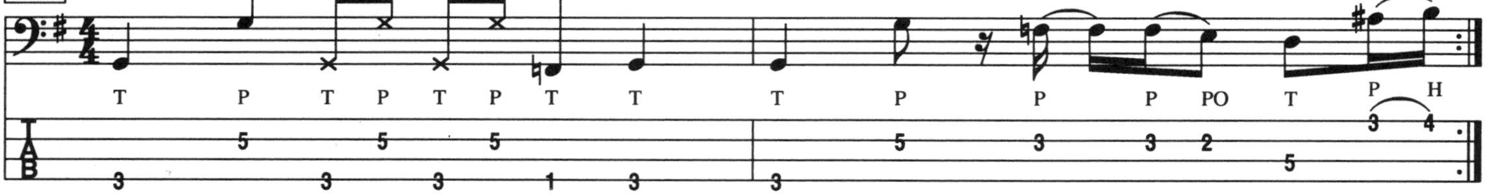

6.34

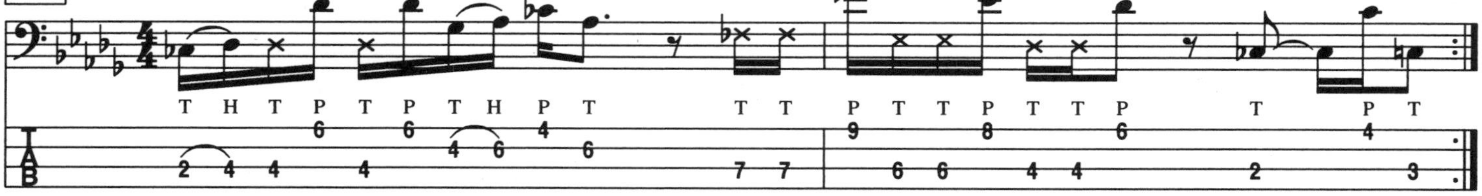

6.35

6.36

6.37

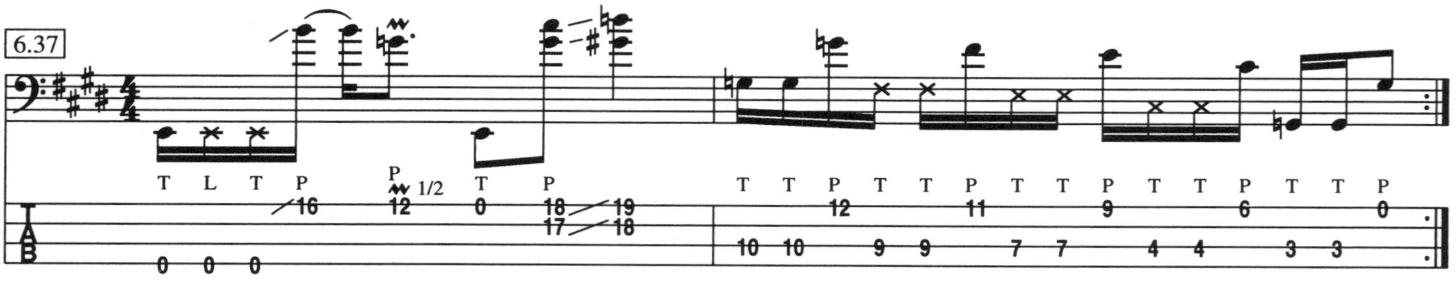

6.38
6.39
6.40
6.41
6.42

6.43

6.44

6.45

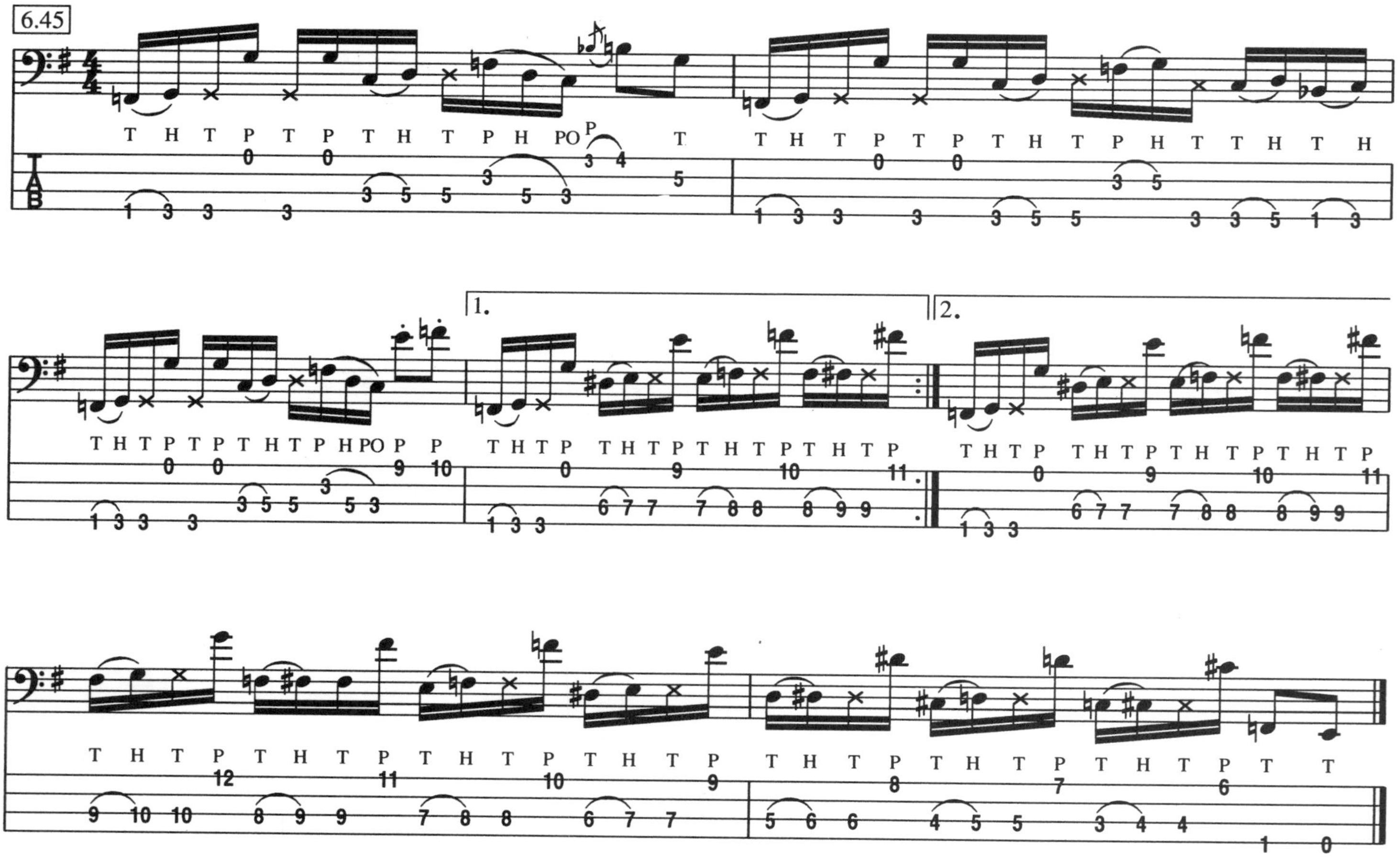

EPILOGUE

Well, you have come a long way. I hope you have been going through the book in order, step by step. If you've skipped over anything (be honest, now, it's just you and me), go back and fill in the gaps. A lot of thought went into organizing this book in the most logical order. Even if you have Chapters 5 and 6 memorized and can play them inside and out, review some of the remedial material once in a while. It will help build your basic skills and strengthen your foundation.

For the last time (I'm going to drill this point home!), **lay down the groove, let the music breathe, do what's expected of you and don't play too much!** Take care of your bass. Groove. Change your strings often. Groove. Make sure you're using the equipment that's right for you. Groove. Practice hard (and properly!). Groove. Become proficient in all twelve keys. Groove. Use your metronome or drum machine. Groove. Use your tape recorder. Groove. If all else fails, smile (but groove!).

Good luck, and happy thumping!

APPENDIX: YOUR EQUIPMENT

Over the past two decades or so, the music world has been inundated with a staggering amount of instruments, gadgetry and general paraphernalia, forcing the musician to make countless decisions about each piece of equipment as he attempts to progress, one step at a time, toward acquiring that "Utopian" set-up. The number of variables existing in a player's outfit these days is infinite. From getting just the "right" sound, feel, look and touch, to obtaining the heaviest, lightest, loudest, quietest, biggest, smallest, highest, lowest, brightest, dullest, most traditional, state-of-the-art piece of gear, the possibilities are limitless.

This Appendix is intended to enlighten the bass player so that he or she can sift intelligently through the overwhelming number of music products available on the market, and cope with the ever-changing technology that faces musicians today. The aspects dealt with in these pages include choosing an instrument, strings, amplifiers, speakers and effects, taking into account the particular needs of the funk bassist.

Though I can offer you information, the choices are ultimately yours. The best thing to do is experiment. Listen to the music I have included in the Discography. Decide just what sound it is you're going for, and try to achieve that sound. Read the trade magazines like *Guitar Player*, *Bass Player*, *Guitar For the Practicing Musician*, *Guitar World*, *Guitar School* etc., and see who's into what. Look at the ads. Hang out at music stores. Check things out. Talk to the guys (and girls) who play the way you'd like to play and find out how they set up their basses, what strings they use and what kind of effects they like (or don't like).

Sometimes they'll list the equipment used on a record. Watch for these kinds of things. Don't allow yourself to be too heavily influenced by product endorsements, though. Buy something because *you* like it, not because your favorite rock star advocates its use.*

Keep your eyes and ears open. Somebody is always coming out with "the latest thing." Try to emulate the "in" sound so people will know you're hip, but at the same time, put a little of yourself into your sound so people will know you're unique.

Make sure you look around long and hard enough to buy intelligently. I always feel better buying name-brand equipment with some kind of warranty. Once you decide what you want, shop around for the best deal. Competition is fierce among music stores. Always try to buy from a reputable dealer who's been around for a long time and won't give you any hassles if something goes wrong. If you have to buy used equipment, first check out the seller and make sure everything smells "kosher" before giving your money to anyone. Take your time and explore your options. Good luck.

YOUR BASS. With so many types of basses available, you'll have many choices about what type of instrument to buy and what features are important to you. It used to be simple: you went out and bought a Fender "Jazz" or a Fender "Precision" bass and an amp (probably an Ampeg B-15) and you had everything you needed because that's all there was! (okay, maybe I'm exaggerating a little, but not that much).

Nowadays we've still got Fenders, but we've also got guys like Michael Tobias, Ken Smith and a few others, who know everything there is to know about every type of wood in the world, from ebony, rosewood and maple to alder, Pernambuco and bubinga. They know which type of tree from which tropical rain forest down in Brazil will make the best neck for getting the most sustain out of a bass when cut in just the right way (this time, I'm *not* exaggerating!). We've also got Alembics, Aria Pro II's, Barringtons, Carvins, Charvels, Clevingers, ESP's, Fernandeses, Foderas, G&Ls, Guilds, Hamers, Hohners, Ibanezes, Kramers, Kubickis, Laravees, Modulus Graphites, Music Mans (Music *Men?*), Peaveys, Pedullas, Pensa-Suhrs, Rickenbackers, Sadowskys, Samicks, Schecters, Spectors, Steinbergers, Tunes, Wals, Warwicks, Washburns, Yamahas, Zetas, Zons and many others. We've got graphite necks and through-the-body necks. We've got four-string, five-string and six-string basses, which can be either fretted, fretless or half-and-half (stop me when you feel I've made my point!). For the technically inclined, we've even got MIDI basses, including Max, Photon and several others.

* Book endorsements are okay, though!

Pick-ups. Certain manufacturers, like EMG, Unisonic and others, have become immensely popular, due to the strength, punchiness, quietness and active electronic circuitry in their pick-ups. Most often these units come in either a "J" (for "Jazz" Bass) or a "P-J" configuration."P-J" stands for "Precision/Jazz," a hybrid configuration which was designed to replace the single pick-up on a Precision Bass with one of the same size, but of superior quality, and also to add a "Jazz" bass pick-up closer to the bridge. This variation allows more high frequencies to pass, as well as more overall sound flexibility. Other high-quality pick-ups include Bartolini, DiMarzio, Schaller, Ken Smith, Sadowsky, and Seymour Duncan. Don't forget to change that little nine-volt battery every once in a while (in the pick-ups that need it). Some "pick-up-less" basses, like the Zetas and a few others, use a bridge pick-up system, eliminating the conventional system of mounted pick-ups.

Bridge. Proper bridge selection is extremely important for sustain, spacing, action and calibration. Maybe you've just got to have a whammy bar. That's okay, too. Most bridges are made of silver-plated brass, which is an excellent material for sustain. Some popular manufacturers of bridges include Badass, DiMarzio, Gotoh, Kahler, Schaller, and others. On many bridges, the saddles are adjustable, so you can vary the spacing between strings. Others must have slots cut into them to secure the strings. These slots are permanent, so make sure whoever cuts the bridge for you knows what they're doing.

Many bridges require a tiny *allen* wrench to adjust the action (height) of each string, and a small screwdriver to adjust the calibration (horizontal movement of the saddle to be sure the bass plays in tune). Unless you want to end up using your nailclippers, make sure you always carry the right tools with you. You never know when your band might get a big gig in some Third World country and you won't feel like braving the town on your own looking for a hardware store (take it from me, it happens!).

Tuning Machines. Make sure your bass has good quality tuning machines that won't get stuck, turn too hard or slip. Grover, Schaller and several other companies make popular machines. The ones on the Modulus Graphite necks turn like butter!

Nut. Another important consideration is the nut (the slotted piece of hardware that secures the strings at the top of the neck). Don't overlook this little device. It's an important part of the bass and can significantly affect the overall tone. Nuts come in brass, ebony, graphite, bone, even plastic (don't buy a plastic nut!). Make sure the nut is the right size for your bass and has the proper spacing between the slots. In some cases, the slots may need to be filed down. Make sure whoever files down the nut is qualified, because it will need to be replaced if it's filed too low.

So what's the best instrument to use for playing funk bass? Since everyone is different, I can't tell you; I can only guide you. I *can* tell you that for slapping and popping, fretted basses are preferred over fretless basses almost a hundred percent of the time because they produce a much "punchier" sound, though exceptions do exist (listen to Paul Simon's "You Can Call Me Al"). The type of bass depends on the player and the circumstances in which he or she is playing. For example, it is not at all uncommon for a studio bassist to take five or more basses to a session. On a prolonged tour of one-nighters, a bassist probably won't afford the luxury of taking more than one or two basses, so he must choose carefully. I find a four-string bass to be the most practical for playing funk. Many five- and six-string basses have very narrow spacing between the strings to avoid making the neck too wide. Steinberger is one extreme. Ken Smith, on the other hand, maintains the four-string spacing on his five- and six-string basses (which have *SUPER WIDE* necks). In some situations, I'll use a five-string if I can get away with it. Sometimes the music is too intricate for the narrower spacing of my five-strings, and I'll end up using a four-string. Four-strings also seem "gutsier" to me for some reason. Active-electronic pick-ups also contribute greatly to the funk sound. It's always nice to have an adjustable bridge, too.

YOUR STRINGS. The next thing you'll need is a good set of strings for your bass. A great many types of strings are available today, so you'll really have to do some experimenting in this department. Flat-wound strings still exist somewhere out there, but stay away from them, especially for playing funk bass. Round-wound strings will give you a much brighter and crisper sound. String gauge is important, too. Most funkers prefer strings gauged on the light side (say, .040, .060, .080 and .100, or often much lighter). I find that the .040s are too light for my taste, and the .045s are too heavy, so I go in between. The strings I use are gauged: .044, .063, .084 and .106 (on my five-strings, I use .130s for the low B's). Not all string manufacturers make these "special" gauges, though. Ken Smith is one that does. Some other quality string manufacturers include D'Addario, Dean Markley, Ernie Ball, Fender, GHS, La Bella, Peavey, Rotosound, S.I.T. and Tobias.

Not only do strings come in a million different gauges, but they also come in short scale, medium scale, long scale and double-ball end (for the Steinbergers and copies). Make sure you get the right type of strings for your bass, and always (*do yourself a favor!*), *ALWAYS* carry spare sets with you. If you aren't always able to have a new set of strings on deck, save the old ones. They just might save your life one night.

YOUR AMPLIFIER AND SPEAKERS. What do you want your amplifier to do? Do you want it to just make you louder? Do you want it to embellish, or otherwise modify your sound? Do you want it to *make* your sound? Do you want it to *be* your sound? Are 50 watts enough? Are 1300 watts enough? What kind of speakers should you use? Do those Bose four-inchers do the trick for you? Maybe you'd like one of those gigantic Ampeg 8 X 10 cabinets. Or how about an SWR 18-inch "Goliath" woofer?

Here we are, facing still more choices. The best advice I can give you is, first, don't skimp on quality. Second, though you can allow a little room for growth, only get what you really need. Overnight sensations are few and far between. Most people who rise to the top do so one step at a time.

Lots of great amps are out on the market these days. SWR and Gallien-Krueger are among the most popular ones with funksters. Trace-Elliot makes some fantastic amps, too. Some people like Walter Woods amps, while others are partial to Acoustic or Peavey. You should also check out Ampeg, Carvin, Crate, Fender, Gibson, Hartke, Marshall, Mesa-Boogie, Pearce, Polytone, Randall, Sunn, Tube Works, and Yamaha.

Your amp should have at least 100 watts of power. Granted, that is pretty low by today's standards, but in most cases it's all you'll need. If you need more, you can find amps with 1,000 watts of power, or even more. The sky's the limit! You don't have to go overboard, though. I've performed at Madison Square Garden and the Shrine Auditorium with 400-watt amps.

As far as amp settings go, there are as many ways to configure those knobs as there are knob configurers. Most funk players tend to boost the low and the high ends, while lowering the midrange. Don't forget all the other variables that go into producing the sound: the player, the bass, strings, effects (we'll get to them in a minute) and speakers. Many other factors exist in determining your settings. Are you playing inside or outside? Are you in a big room or a small one? Is the room full or (Heaven forbid!) empty? Does the room have a high ceiling? Wooden floors? Carpeting? Is it a "dead" room or a "live" room? You've got to consider everything and act accordingly.

The speaker you use with your amp can make or break your rig. Since it's the last step through which your sound passes, it's your "last chance" at getting that great sound.

I wasn't kidding when I mentioned four-inch speakers for bass. Bose 802s are made up of eight 4-inch speakers per cabinet, and some bass players (mostly upright players) swear by them. I wouldn't recommend them for our purposes, but if you want to try them, maybe you'll like them! Electro-Voice and JBL still make great speakers and will probably be around forever. Hartke and SWR cabinets have become enormously popular over the last few years. I definitely wouldn't buy a speaker before testing it. Gauss is another speaker worth auditioning. You should also check out Bold Concepts, Genz-Benz and Sonic. Many more are available, too. Check them all out!

Now let's take a look at some speaker types and sizes. It's important to make your bass sound good in all registers. You need that low, boomy (but not *too* boomy) tone on the bottom, and that extra crispness and percussiveness at the top. Boosting the highs helps you give the *lower* register that "punchiness" that partly epitomizes the funk sound. You'll also need a certain amount of midrange (not too much, please) to add a little body.

So what kind of speaker(s) will give us that ultimate funk bass sound in all registers from rock-bottom "B" to stratosphere "C?" Start experimenting! Bass speaker technology is about as sophisticated as you could want. Try bi-amping or tri-amping. Or just use a 12-inch speaker in a good cabinet. How about four 10-inch speakers? I had a cabinet built once with a 15-inch JBL speaker and a horn, which I liked very much.

Some companies, like Hartke, SWR and others, offer a variety of speaker configurations, which can be combined in many ways. Among the most common set-ups are cabinets with either one 15-inch speaker, two 10-inch speakers or four 10-inch speakers. Many bassists, like Will Lee and Darryl Jones, get a large part of their sound by using combinations of these three configurations.

SWR recently came out with their "Goliath" line, which has some really nice features. They have a 4-10 cabinet with a "bullet" in the middle controlled by a knob in the back of the cabinet (they also make the same cabinet with two 10s). The bullet can be completely off, completely on, or anywhere in between. It's very practical. The Goliath line also includes an 18-inch woofer for those low lows. Genz-Benz is another company that manufactures great sounding speakers with a bullet in the middle.

Many speakers, including the Goliaths, enable you to get more power out of your amp because they have impedances of 4-ohms, instead of the more common 8-ohms. Be careful when you start changing impedance levels on your amp. You can cause some serious damage if you don't know what you're doing. A quick rule to remember: the output impedance rating of the amp should be the same or lower than the impedance rating of the speaker, but it should never be higher than the speaker rating.

YOUR EFFECTS. It's easy to go overboard in this department, and most people do. Don't get caught up in the arms race to see who can accumulate the biggest, deadliest, most "awesome" arsenal of toys.

Following is a list of effects, devices and gadgets that are in common use today, followed by a brief description of each one. Of course words alone cannot describe these effects, so make sure you get your hands (and ears) on them for yourself, and do lots of experimenting. Many more effects are available, but the ones here are the most common.

Volume Pedal. Let's start with an easy one. Volume pedals are great for controlling the strength of the signal going to your amp when you just can't stop playing, not even for an eighth note. They also allow you to play more expressively. Some run on batteries, some have AC power cords and others require no external power source at all. Many volume pedals are coupled with a "wah-wah" effect. Test out any volume pedal before you buy it and make sure it feels comfortable, moves smoothly and is sensitive (but not *too* sensitive) to subtle movements. Also, it should have some kind of rubber feet or "stoppers" on the bottom to keep it from sliding around while you play. Volume pedals run about $50 to $60 and up. Once you start using one, you'll wonder how you ever got along without it.

Tuner. *Not really an effect, but let's just say your music will sound more effective if you play in tune.* A quartz tuner is a very handy device to have. It shows you if you're in tune, even if you can't actually hear yourself (try asking everyone in the room to be quiet for a minute so you can tune your bass, and see what kind of reaction you get!). They typically sell for less than $100, often quite a bit less. You don't always get what you pay for so be careful. I once purchased one of the "better" quartz tuners and found it to be about ten cents sharp.

Most tuners have a little microphone. This feature is handy for singers, woodwind and brass players, etc. Also, many tuners allow you to change the "reference" pitch from A-440 to, say, A-442 or even A-445.

Especially in the studio, there's a big difference between playing in tune and playing *incredibly* in tune. Some studios are equipped with strobe tuners which are even more accurate than quartz tuners. Keep in mind that the tuner is just a tool and a guide. Although technology has come a long way, your *ear* is always the final judge.

OK, ready to get down to the good stuff? Just be careful you don't overdo it and get in over your head, especially when the guy at the music store, or the guy down the block, tells you you've got to have a GTX/280Z-50 or you're just not with it. Effects are important. They're just more important to some people than to others. On the one hand we have players like Steve Swallow and Victor Bailey, who use little or no effects and depend on their hands to get their sound (what a concept!). On the other hand, we've got guys like Mark Egan, who owns at least one of everything! Each piece of equipment Mark has, though, was acquired for a specific reason, because he knows what he's doing and he's constantly thinking of "the big picture." What sound(s) are you going for, and how will each variable in your chain of processors affect your overall sound? If you've just gotta have a GTX/280Z-50, so be it!

In most cases, the effects described below are available either in rack-mountable modules or "stomp boxes" (pedals that are turned on and off by stepping on them). Virtually all of them are available in mono, stereo or "simulated stereo." Guitar and bass players have traditionally favored the stomp boxes over rack-mounts, but that trend may be changing. The rack-mounts are often less noisy, and in most cases, of higher quality than the stomp boxes. Also, some of the rack-mounts provide up to twelve effects at once. Furthermore, now that MIDI is here, parameters, patch changes and overall sounds can be changed on the rack-mounts via a MIDI foot pedal.

This technology can get expensive. What's more, many die-hard guitar players just love their stomp boxes and wouldn't trade them for anything. As I've said before, it's up to you. Some good quality manufacturers of effects include: A.D.A., Alesis, Aphex, A.R.T., Boss, DBX, Digitech, D.O.D, Eventide, Furman, Hughes & Kettner, Korg, Lexicon, Rane, Rocktron, Roland, S.D.E., Yamaha and many others.

Delay. Here's an effect that has grown tremendously popular among bass players over the past several years, especially for fretlesses. A delay reproduces and repeats the sound of your bass anywhere from a few milliseconds to as much as over seven seconds later. Originally, delays were achieved by using a tape recorder to get a time delay between the "record" and the "playback" heads. Soon afterward analog delays came into popular use.

Today, tape and analog delays have given way to digital delays. Digital delays (or DDLs, as we say in the biz) offer extremely clean sound and faithful reproduction at a fraction of the cost.

Chorus. A chorus is one effect that I recommend quite highly, as it can greatly enhance the funk bass sound. This processor electronically delays and varies the pitch of the output signal above and below that of the input signal. As the two signals are blended together, your ear perceives the two sounds as having been made at the same time, thus creating a wavy, multiple-voice effect. Chorusing is best appreciated in stereo, with the processed signal coming out of one speaker and the unprocessed signal out of the other.

Flanger. A flanger is another form of modulated delay. It copies the signal, delays it, varies the pitch and then mixes the delayed signal back with the original signal. The delay time, however, is usually much shorter than in a chorus. What's more, a portion of the processed sound can be redirected back into the input for further processing, resulting in a feedback loop. This feedback gives the flanger its distinctive swishing and whooshing effect. Flanging was originally done with two tape recorders, by increasing and decreasing the speed of one of the reels, while the other remained constant. This technique was known as a "reel flange."

Reverb. Though this effect is not as common among bassists as it is for, well, *everyone* else, it's such a "biggie" in today's sound that it just can't be overlooked.

Reverb devices can be divided into four basic types: spring, plate, chamber and (what else?) digital. Spring reverb was the culprit all those times you (and I) bumped the Twin Reverb or the Vocal Master and caused what sounded like an explosion. Plate reverb, once common in recording studios, involved a suspended plate with a transducer in the middle. Chamber reverb was created in a specially designed "acoustic room," often made of concrete or shellacked material, with no parallel walls.

Digital, as you may have guessed, is the most common type of reverb used in music today. It is extremely flexible in that it can vary the decay time, EQ (equalization — we're coming to that next), crossover points and all kinds of other really neat technical stuff. Most digital reverb units have memory presets, so you can "call up" your favorite reverb type by pushing a button or two. Your reverb unit will probably have settings called "small hall," "medium hall," "concert hall," etc. Often they get pretty fancy, too, with effects like "reverse reverb," "gated reverb," "reverse gated reverb," and so on. Some of the very sophisticated digital reverb units in recording studios can simulate spring, plate and chamber reverbs, as well (you see, producers always have to have just the right reverb on the snare drum and will usually go to any expense to get it!).

Equalizer. Equalizers are very practical devices to have, and can drastically alter your overall sound. An equalizer, or *EQ*, isolates a particular frequency (or range of frequencies) so that it can be either boosted or cut. Basically, EQs come in two types: graphic and parametric. A graphic EQ allows you to control only one very specific frequency at a time. It is composed of a series of slider faders, which are actually like volume controls. Each fader is assigned to a frequency (eg., 63Hz*, 500Hz, 8KHz), referred to as a "band," and hovers around a central point of reference. When you slide the fader up, the level of that frequency is raised; when you slide it down, it's lowered. In the middle it's "flat." Graphic EQs are available from about 5-band up to 32-band. Obviously, the more bands you have, the more precisely you can manipulate your sound. They come in mono, stereo and, yes, digital.

Parametric EQs can determine the actual band*width.* Instead of boosting, say, just 10K, you can boost everything between 8.5K and 11K. Since this type of EQ is so versatile, it doesn't require a lot of bands. In fact I've recorded on $750,000 consoles that had only 4-band quasi-parametric EQs. I've also seen high-quality rack-mountable parametric EQ units, with *five* bands, for only about $350.

Other types of EQ include high-pass filters, low-pass filters, notch filters, even something called a "paragraphic" EQ. Most digital equalizers can create all kinds of EQ, often combining two or more kinds simultaneously. Check out all your options and see what you like (and need).

* Hz is the abbreviation for Hertz, meaning cycles per second. K is short for KHz, which stands or Kilohertz. One Kilohertz = 1,000 Hertz, or 1,000 cycles per second.

Compressor/Limiter. A compressor makes soft sounds louder and loud sounds softer. Virtually every major recording studio has some type of compressor/limiter. It can be a terrific enhancement to your funk bass sound, whether in the studio or on the gig. The effect narrows your range of volume, or "squashes" your sound. For example, if sometimes you're playing at 30dB (dB stands for decibels, the units for measuring volume) and sometimes you're playing at 120dB, you can use a compressor to shrink that audio range and keep everything between, say, 50dB and 90dB.

Here's how it works: When your input volume level exceeds a certain level (called a "threshold"), the compressor steps in and lowers the output signal. The amount by which the signal is lowered is determined by the "compression ratio." A compression ratio of 5:1 (five-to-one) tells the compressor to raise the output by 1 dB for every 5 dB of input. If the quiet parts are too quiet, the overall level can be increased by turning up the "output" knob. The desired sound is attained by varying the compression ratio and the output level.

When the compression ratio is large enough, the compressor becomes a *limiter*. The job of a limiter is to prevent the signal from going too high, usually to avoid overloading amps or other equipment. Typical compression ratios for limiters are 10:1 and 20:1, though they could go much higher. Radio stations, for example, use "brick wall" limiting, which is boosting their signals as high as possible, without having to worry about broadcasting beyond their licensed power ratings.

Noise gate. This device works on the same principle as a compressor. It has a threshold level, below which it won't "kick in." In other words, unless it receives a certain level of input (dBs), it will cut off any sounds in the signal flow. Noise gates are very practical for eliminating a hum or a high-pitched "hiss" that may be audible between musical phrases during quiet passages.

Other Effects. Most of the important effects have been covered, but here are a few more sounds you might want to investigate: *Aural Exciter, Distortion, Harmonizer, Heavy Metal, Octave Divider, Overdrive, Pitch Changer, Phase Shifter, Vibrato* and *Wah-Wah*.

As I stated at the beginning, the intent of this Appendix is to expose you to some of the equipment used by people in the music industry today (bass players in particular), and to offer some insights into what you may (or may *not*) need. I hope now you'll be able to choose carefully and buy more intelligently, without going too far, or getting talked into spending thousands of dollars on things you really don't need. Input from others is helpful, but when it comes down to choosing *your* equipment, decide for yourself what it will take to do the trick. Who knows? You may even decide to buy only a Fender "Precision" and an Ampeg B-15. The novelty of it just might work!

DISCOGRAPHY

Music is all about sound and about hearing. Being able to read it is one thing, but *hearing* it is crucial to understanding it, and imitating it expands your horizons and helps you grow. The cassette tape that accompanies this book (and I hope you've been using it!) is necessary for getting down the basic concepts of funk bass, but is, for the most part, taken out of context. Following is a list of bass players, many of whom are among the greatest in the world, and a sampling of some of their recordings of funk bass. Listen and imitate (repeat as necessary).

<u>Jimmy Allen</u>
"You're the One" w/Henry Johnson, MCA 5754

<u>Scott Ambush</u>
"Rhythm Deep" w/Omar Hakim, GRP 9585

<u>Victor Bailey</u>
"Bottom's Up" Atlantic 81978
"Inferno" w/Birelli Lagrene, Blue Note BLJ-48016

<u>Brian Bromberg</u>
"Basses Loaded" Intima D2-73325
"Magic Rain" Intima 7 7352
"Bassically Speaking" Nova 9031

<u>Baron Browne</u>
"Warning" w/Billy Cobham, GRP 9528
"Power Play" w/Billy Cobham, GRP 9536

<u>Bunny Brunel</u>
"Ivanhoe" Inner City IC 1162

<u>Oscar Cartaya</u>
"Point of View" w/Spyro Gyra, MCA 6309
"Fast Forward" w/Spyro Gyra, GRP 9608

<u>Stanley Clarke</u>
"Stanley Clarke" Epic EK 36973
"Journey To Love" Epic 36974
"School Days" Epic EK 36975

<u>Bootsy Collins</u>
"What's Bootsy Doin'?" Columbia CK 44107

<u>Randy Coven</u>
"Funk Me Tender" Guitar Recordings 88561-5011-2
"Sammy Says Ouch" Guitar Recordings 88561-5030-2

<u>Nathan East</u>
"Every Step of the Way" w/David Benoit, GRP 9558
"This Side Up" w/David Benoit, En Pointe ENP 0001
"The Sky Is the Limit" w/Alphonse Mouzon, Pausa PR 7173

Kai Eckhardt
"Fiafiaga" w/Vital Information, Columbia CK 44334
"Live at the Royal Festival Hall" w/John McLaughlin Trio, JMT 834 436

Bob Feldman
"This Side Up" w/David Benoit, En Pointe ENP 0001

Ronnie Garrett
"Never Too Much" w/Henry Johnson, MCA 6329

Lincoln Goines
"Urban Contours" w/Bob Mintzer, DMP CD-467
"Kalahari" w/Dave Valentin, GRP 9508
"Jungle Garden" w/Dave Valentin, GRP 9523
"Light Struck" w/Dave Valentin, GRP 9537
"Mind Time" w/Dave Valentin, GRP 9554

Larry Graham
"Graham Central Station" Warner Bros. B-2763
"Release Yourself" w/Graham Central Station, Warner Bros. B-2814
"Ain't No Doubt About It" w/Graham Central Station, Warner Bros. B-2876
"Mirror" w/Graham Central Station, Warner Bros. B-2973
"Now Do-U-Wanta Dance" w/Graham Central Station, Warner Bros. BS 3041
"My Radio Sure Sounds Good To Me" w/Graham Central Station, Warner Bros. BSK 3175
"Star Walk" w/Graham Central Station, Warner Bros. K-3322
"Victory" Warner Bros. 9 23878

Gary Grainger
"Blue Matter" w/John Scofield, Gramavision 18-8702
"Loud Jazz" w/John Scofield, Gramavision 18-8801
"Pick Hits Live" w/The John Scofield Band, Gramavision 18-8805

Stuart Hamm
"Radio Free Albemuth" Relativity 88561-8209
"Kings Of Sleep" Relativity 88561-1013
"The Urge" Relativity 88561-1052

Jimmy Haslip
"Yellowjackets" Warner Bros., BSK 3573
"Mirage À Trois" w/Yellowjackets, Warner Bros., 9 23813
"Shades" w/Yellowjackets, MCA 5752

Jonas Hellborg
"Mahavishnu" w/John McLaughlin, Warner Bros. 9 25190

Neil Jason
"Don't Stop the Music" w/The Brecker Brothers, Arista 4122
"The Brecker Brothers Collection/Volume One" Novus 3075-2-N
"Heavy Metal Be-Bop" w/The Brecker Brothers, Arista AB 4185
"Why Do Fools Fall In Love?" w/Diana Ross, RCA AFL1-4153
"Silk Electric" w/Diana Ross, RCA 4384-2 R11 (CD), 4384-4 R6 (Cassette)
"Hideaway" w/David Sanborn, Warner Bros. BSK 3379
"NY Cats Direct" w/John Tropea DMP CD-453

Louis Johnson
"Light Up the Night" w/The Brothers Johnson, A&M SP-3716
"Winners" w/The Brothers Johnson, A&M SP-3724
"Right On Time" w/The Brothers Johnson, A&M SP-4644
"Out Of Control" w/The Brothers Johnson, A&M SP-4965
"The Brothers Johnson" 25th Anniversary Classics, Vol. 11, A&M CD 2509
"Kickin'" w/The Brothers Johnson, A&M CD 5162/DX 1684
"Living Inside Your Love" w/Earl Klugh, Blue Note BN-LA667-G
"The Dude" w/Quincy Jones, A&M SP-3248
"Time Exposure" w/Stanley Clarke, Epic 38688

Darryl "The Munch" Jones
"Decoy" w/Miles Davis, Columbia FC 38991
"You're Under Arrest" w/Miles Davis, Columbia CK 40023

Mark King
"Influences" Polydor 823 088
"Level 42" w/Level 42 Polydor 821 935
"True Colours" w/Level 42, Polydor 823 542
"A Physical Presence" w/Level 42, Polydor 825677

Abraham Laboriel
"More Than A Feelin'" w/Koinonia, Sparrow 1076
"Celebration" w/Koinonia, Sparrow 1093
"Frontline" w/Koinonia, Sparrow 1116
"Picture This" w/Billy Cobham, GRP 9551
"Migration" w/Dave Grusin, GRP 9592
"For My Friends" w/Greg Mathieson, Headfirst A215
"Jarreau" w/Al Jarreau, Warner Bros. 23801
"Last Nite" w/Larry Carlton, MCA 5866
"The Immigrants" w/The Zawinul Syndicate, Columbia CK 40969
"Birds of Passage" w/Sadao Watanabe, Elektra 9 60748
"Carmel" w/Joe Sample, MCA 37210 (CD), 1684 (Cassette)

Tim Landers
"Orion" w/Vital Information, Columbia FC 39375
"Global Beat" w/Vital Information, Columbia CK 40506
"Fiafiaga" w/Vital Information, Columbia CK 44334
"GRP Super Live Concert" w/Grusin, Ritenour & Scott, GRP 2-1650

Dave Larue
"Southern Steel" w/The Steve Morse Band, MCA 10112

Will Lee
"The Brecker Brothers Collection/Volume One" Novus 3075-2-N
"Living Inside Your Love" w/Earl Klugh, Blue Note BN-LA667-G
"From All Sides" w/Hiram Bullock, Atlantic 7 81685
"Give It What U Got" w/Hiram Bullock, Atlantic 7 81790
"Catching the Sun" w/Spyro Gyra, MCA 5108
"Freetime" w/Spyro Gyra, MCA 5238
"Foxie" w/Bob James, Columbia/Tappan Zee FC 38801

Marcus Miller

"Winelight" w/Grover Washington, Jr., Elektra 6E-305
"Never Too Much" w/Luther Vandross Epic FE 37451
"Rit" w/Lee Ritenour, GRP 9524
"Night Lines" w/Dave Grusin, GRP 9504
"As We Speak" w/David Sanborn, Warner Bros. 9 23650
"Backstreet" w/David Sanborn, Warner Bros. 9 23906
"Voyeur" w/David Sanborn, Warner Bros. BSK 3544
"Straight To the Heart" w/David Sanborn, Warner Bros. 9 25150
"Double Vision" w/Bob James & David Sanborn, Warner Bros. 9 25393
"A Change of Heart" w/David Sanborn, Warner Bros. 9 25479
"Close-Up" w/David Sanborn, Reprise 9 25715
"The Man With the Horn" w/Miles Davis, Columbia FC 36790
"Amandla" w/Miles Davis, Warner Bros. 9 25873
"Spellbound" w/Joe Sample, Warner Bros. 9 25781
"Ashes to Ashes" w/Joe Sample, Warner Bros. W2 26318
"The Hawk" w/Dave Valentin, GRP 9515
"Healing the Wounds" w/The Crusaders, GRP 9638

John Patitucci

"John Patitucci" GRP 9560
"On the Corner" GRP 9583
"Sketchbook" GRP 9617
"The Chick Corea Elektric Band" GRP 9535
"Light Years" w/Chick Corea, GRP 9546
"Eye Of the Beholder" w/Chick Corea, GRP 9564
"Inside Out" w/Chick Corea, GRP 9601
"Beneath the Mask" w/Chick Corea, GRP 9649
"GRP Super Live Concert" w/Chick Corea, GRP 2-1650
"Voices of the Heart" w/Eric Marienthal, GRP 9563
"Oasis" w/Eric Marienthal, GRP 9655
"The Other Side Of The Story" w/Brandon Fields, Nova 8602-2

Frank Russell

"You're the One" w/Henry Johnson, MCA 5754
"Never Too Much" w/Henry Johnson, MCA 6329

ACKNOWLEDGMENTS

Sure, I'd like to take all the credit for writing this book. Truth is, though, I had help. A lot of people went out of their way to help me make this project (and it *was* a project!) move more smoothly, easily and efficiently. I'd like to take this opportunity to acknowledge these people's generosity.

Thanks to the musicians who took the time to talk with me, read my manuscript and actually come up with good things to say about my book:

- **John Patitucci**: I don't know where you found the time to hang out, John, but I sure do appreciate it. Even though I did have to sit and watch you rehearse your incredible band while waiting to talk to you, *really*, I didn't mind! Thanks for putting up with all the trans-global phone calls and faxes (what an age we live in!). Thanks for going so far out of your way to help me. Much luck and continued success to you.

- **Rich Appleman**: A true pedagogue! Thanks for your support and encouragement. Berklee is lucky to have you.

- **Brian Bromberg**: Glad the word finally got out about what a great player and writer you are. Hell, I've known that for years! Thanks, man.

- **Bob Cranshaw**: I admire your meticulous, no-nonsense, down-to-business approach. Thank you.

- **Mark Egan**: I didn't mind sitting through your rehearsal, either! Thanks.

- **Stuart Hamm:** I am truly honored to have been the one chosen to transcribe the music for your Hal Leonard book. Throughout the ordeal, though, you quickly went from being my mentor to my *tor*mentor! Seriously, I appreciate all the time we got to spend working together. Now let's go eat!

- **Neil Jason**: What can I say, Neil? You helped me make the phone company rich! Thanks for all your suggestions, and thanks for being a great guy!

- **Will Lee**: You sure are hard to get a hold of, but it was definitely worth the effort! Thank you!

Thanks to all my friends, "consultants" and experts in their respective fields:

- Alexis Sklarevski, Dale Titus and everyone at the Bass Institute of Technology, Hollywood, California
- Don Coffman, Director of Jazz Bass at the University of Miami School of Music, Coral Gables, Florida
- Tim Emmons and Todd Ferguson at the Dick Grove School of Music, Van Nuys, California
- Dennis Tini, Matt Michaels, Gary Leach and Dan Pliskow of the Jazz Studies Department at Wayne State University, Detroit
- Sid Beshkin: The world's foremost authority on print technology!
- Steve Carryer, Cliff Cohen and Tom Hollyer: three of the most amazing Macintosh wizards on the planet!
- "Dr. Jazz" of Dr. Jazz Operations, Oak Park, Michigan
- Mike "Friedbaum" Friedman. He's my "Mr. Drummer Friend" (see Chapter 1). Thanks for working out all those grooves with me, dude.
- Abe Laboriel: A great inspiration and a true gentleman (*and what a bass player!*). Thanks for your help and encouragement.
- Herb Mickman: Hey, Herb. Did you hear the one about...?
- Steve Shepard and everyone at Scorpion Systems Group (the "Sybil" people)
- The staff of the Specs Howard School of Broadcast Arts, Southfield, Michigan
- The staff of PM Productions, Southfield, Michigan

Thanks to my merciless proofreaders: Marty Liebman (yo, Bro!), Tom Profit and Rey Sanchez.
Thanks to John Cerullo, Joff Jones and everyone at Hal Leonard Publishing Corporation.

Thanks to Sammi and Josh.

Special thanks to Rey Sanchez (see merciless proofreaders, above). Actually, I don't know whether to thank him, or to blame him! If it weren't for Rey, it never would have occurred to me to write a book (thanks a lot!). That night in Bogota, Colombia — was it just a suggestion when you said, "Hey, man, you ought to write a book. A funk book. Yeah, that's it. A funk book," or was it a dare? Well anyway, here it is! Thanks for the huge hand you've had in my success — all the gigs, all the tours, all those times in the studio. Thanks for introducing me to Jaco. Thanks for your friendship. Where are we going, next?

ABOUT THE AUTHOR

Jon Liebman holds a Bachelor of Music degree in Jazz Studies and Contemporary Media from Wayne State University in Detroit, and a Master of Music degree in Studio Music and Jazz from the University of Miami in Coral Gables, Florida. He has performed extensively throughout world, playing electric and acoustic bass for everything from jazz gigs and club dates to national television shows and full-scale concerts at Madison Square Garden. He has also played in the pit orchestras of many Broadway shows, including *Ain't Misbehavin', Into the Woods, Fame, Golden Boy, Dreamgirls* and *Phantom of the Opera.*

Jon has toured with jazz greats Cleo Laine and Buddy De Franco, and has played bass for The Fifth Dimension, The Coasters, The Ink Spots, The Chiffons, Billy Eckstine, Eartha Kitt, Jose Feliciano, Jerry Vale, Julio Iglesias and many others. He has also recorded numerous records, demos, soundtracks, films and industrial shows, including several projects for Ford, General Motors and the NBA.

As a writer, Jon has been commissioned countless times to write arrangements for musical ensembles of all types and sizes. Two of his big-band arrangements have been performed on The Tonight Show and The Late Show (forerunner of the Arsenio Hall show). He has also worked as a music proofreader and copyist. In addition to Funk Bass, Jon is also the author of a book of transcriptions of the music of fellow bassist Stuart Hamm.

Jon has spent time in California, as well, having been very active in the Los Angeles music scene as a performer and writer. He now makes his home in Southfield, Michigan, where he works as a studio bassist, writer and producer.

ENDORSEMENTS

"I have never seen a better book from which to learn this style. I recommend Funk Bass to all 'slappers' and 'wanna-be slappers.' It's a can't miss!"

- John Patitucci
Bassist with Chick Corea
GRP Recording Artist

"This book provides a good basis for what funk is really made of!"

- Will Lee
Bassist of "Late Night with David Letterman"

"Well done, Jon! One of the most thorough books on "slapping" and "popping" ever written! Funk Bass covers everything from the basics to the finer points, all in a very easy to understand and entertaining way. I would feel good about recommending this book to anyone who wants to learn this style of bass playing!

- Stuart Hamm
Bassist with Steve Vai, Joe Satriani
Relativity Recording Artist

"An excellent approach for the serious player who wants to get the slapping technique together. From beginner to advanced, this book is a valuable tool."

- Mark Egan
Bassist with Sting, Elements
Novus recording artist

"A great study for musicians looking to learn, or improve upon, their slap technique."

- Neil Jason
Bassist with Roxy Music, David Sanborn, Diana Ross

"This is an informative book covering various aspects of the funk/slapping technique. I especially like the section on equipment and effects. This is very useful information!"

- Brian Bromberg
Bassist with Lee Ritenour, Billy Cobham
Nova recording artist

"Very informative for this contemporary style of bass playing. Includes basic, fundamental material, as well as the more advanced topics. Includes much valuable written information in addition to the music. This is the first time I have ever seen all this type of information assembled in one source. I would recommend this book to all those bassists interested in the funk style of playing."

- Rich Appleman
Chairman: Bass Department
Berklee College of Music

"An excellent primer for the thumb because the explanations are very clear and concise . . . excellent information for practice and performance. This book also includes great instructions and excellent advice. Thumbs up!"

- Bob Cranshaw
New York Studio Legend